Creative Financing Handbook For Real Estate Professionals

Gary Chefetz

Copyright 2025
Gary Chefetz

Publisher: Investor Allies Inc.
124 Via Tuscany, Rancho Mirage CA 92270

Book Download: creativefinaningbook.com

gary@creativefinancingbook.com

Library of Congress Cataloging-in-Publication Data

Creative Financing Handbook for Real Estate Professionals/ Gary Chefetz

1. Real estate 2. Real estate business 3. Real estate investment

ISBN: 979-8-9991610-0-0

Printed in the U.S.A.

This publication is designed to provide up to date and authoritative infor-mation related to the subject matter. The reader is cautioned to verify any law citations or summaries contained herein and to seek advice of counsel prior to making legally consequential decisions based on the content of this publication

Edition A

Table of Contents

Foreword

If you are a licensed real estate agent, let me say this clearly: you are sitting on the single greatest opportunity of your career but only if you are willing to break free from the old way of doing things.

The traditional real estate model is broken. Too many listings expire. Too many families get turned away. Too many agents walk from deals just because the bank said no. In my world, we don't walk we restructure. We solve problems. We close gaps that others leave wide open. And now, for the first time, there is a book written specifically to help real estate agents step into that world.

This book by Gary Chefetz is more than a guide. It is a tactical, honest, no-fluff playbook written by someone who understands the realities of agency law, brokerage policy, and creative deal-making. Gary doesn't just teach theory. He operates in the trenches. He knows what it takes to structure deals that work, while protecting your license and serving your clients at the highest level. That's what makes this book so powerful. It's not just another regurgitation of YouTube content or social media scripts. It's smart, direct, and built for the working agent.

And the truth is this: agents who refuse to adapt are going to be left behind. AI is already doing your CMAs. Wholesalers are calling your expired listings. Sellers want results, not excuses. The market is shifting, and the old tools simply are not enough. You need more in your toolbox. Creative finance is that tool. It is the tool that keeps deals alive when nothing else works.

In my Sub To community, I have watched hundreds of licensed agents double their income and impact not by working harder, but by thinking differently. They are structuring subject-to deals, wraps, novation, and seller finance transactions. They are saving deals, helping families, and building reputations as problem solvers not just order takers.

So, if you are reading this, it means you are ready. Ready to see real estate through a new lens. Ready to stop walking away from opportunities and start creating new ones. Whether this is your launchpad into creative finance or the sharpening stone that takes your skills to the next level, this book is a gift to the industry, and Gary Chefetz is the perfect person to deliver it.

Now let's go close some creative deals.

Pace Morby
Founder, SubTo

Acknowledgements

First and foremost, I thank my friend Pace Morby not only for his kind words and willingness to share them as a foreword, but most emphatically for creating the Sub To community. The transactional experience and insights required to write this book I gained from working with investors in the community. If not for the Sub To community, this book would not exist. Now, after five years immersed in this extraordinary culture, I can state without hesitation that the experience is transformational.

My thanks also to the Wagoner Law Firm, P.L.L.C. of Wilmington North Carolina for sharing their custom GPT, U.S. Law. This accelerated the legal research required to infuse the text with important examples of state laws and the impact of variances from state to state. Note that you should use this tool to find statutes and references rather than to interpret them. Keep in mind that Chat GPT makes mistakes!

Finally, my sincerest thanks to my clients for continuously challenging me with their real estate deals. Every creative financing deal is a learning opportunity. Each has its own unique circumstances, obstacles, and personalities. Although we may not be able to close every deal, we accumulate knowledge working through each one.

Introduction

As a real estate investor and now as an agent who specializes in working with investors, I realized that there is a knowledge gap between agents who work with primary homebuyers and agents who routinely work with investors who focus on residential properties. The purpose of this book is to bridge that gap enabling agents like you to expand your opportunity market.

If your marketing game is already sustaining you by landing buyers and sellers who change homes once every five to ten years, imagine how adding clients who purchase five to ten properties annually. can transform your bottom line. While it is true that you may need to adjust your fees for your frequent fliers, dramatically lower client acquisition cost can offset that adjustment.

To embrace and serve the investor psyche, you must understand the power of leverage. The core learning in this text is alternative financing and creative deal structures that help real estate investors grow their portfolio with the least amount of cash.

As a listing agent, when you adopt this knowledge, it should quickly become apparent to you that there are details about your listings that you simply do not know. Important details! Details that might make an enormous difference in how much your seller stands to net, and details that could potentially shorten days on the market.

As a buyer's agent when you dig in deeper you become aware of strategies that allow you to find solutions for clients that you might have written off in the past. The strategies presented in this book allow you to solve more problems for buyers and sellers.

If you are an investor, there are plenty of golden nuggets in this book for you, too, such as giving a copy to your favorite agent or broker, especially one who struggles to understand your creative financing offers!

xvii

Chapter 1:
Creative Finance Matters Now

Creative finance is the art of structuring real estate solutions, often applying, but not limited to, scenarios outside traditional lending and institutional boundaries. It is not a loophole, gimmick, or sleight of hand. Rather, it is a set of principled, flexible approaches that solve real problems for buyers and sellers in dynamic markets. By mastering these methods, you position yourself to:

- Resolve more client obstacles with agility.
- Expand the pool of eligible buyers for listings.
- Increase homeownership viability for individuals overlooked by conventional financing.

Creative finance is not an alternative for when deals are desperate. It is a proactive strategy for agents and brokers who wish to lead, not follow, in a rapidly transforming industry.

The Changing Landscape of Real Estate Practice

The real estate profession is not what it was even five years ago. Today, agents and brokers face a dual challenge: emerging competition and disruptive technology.

The rise of wholesaling siphons momentum from traditional channels. Wholesalers, often operating without licenses, move contracts without owning property, frequently bypassing agency relationships altogether. They promise speed and flexibility that agents must now match to remain relevant.

Artificial intelligence can replicate the advisory role once exclusive to agents. From automated valuation models to AI-driven listing descriptions and virtual transaction assistants, technology increasingly delivers what consumers used to rely on you to provide. You must evolve or be edged out.

Why This Knowledge Is Timely

Market conditions are tightening. High interest rates, economic uncertainty, and affordability crises are converging. Deals are falling apart more frequently, and standard financing fails to meet the moment.

In June 2024, approximately 56,000 home-purchase agreements were canceled. In total 14.9% of all transactions initiated that month making it the highest cancellation rate for any June on record (Redfin, 2024). Existing home sales in the United States fell to their lowest level since 1995, dropping to an annualized rate of just 4.06 million in 2024 (MarketWatch, 2024). Although home prices remain high, seller profit margins are shrinking, with the typical return on investment declining for the second year to 53.8% (ATTOM Data Solutions, 2024). The year 2025 promises to maintain those trends and with economic uncertainty the new normal, the market could take unexpected turns.

Traditional finance models are straining under these pressures. Creative finance offers pathways where conventional methods fail. For example, in 2024, an investor I worked with acquired a property using a subject-to strategy, taking over an existing mortgage at a locked-in rate of 2.75% while new mortgage rates had climbed beyond 7%. That differential in the interest rate made the investment feasible and highlights precisely why deal structure, not just pricing, determines outcomes.

When you know how to structure a seller carryback, navigate a subject-to transaction, or build a wraparound mortgage, you can keep a deal alive that others let die. You transform from a transactional agent into a strategic problem solver.

How I Acquired My First Multi-Unit Without Full Financing

In my early twenties, I launched a successful periodical publishing business. After the first year of publishing my flagship entertainment magazine, I needed a permanent location for my thriving team and expanding operations. I identified an ideal location, but the building owner refused to contribute to the buildout or offer a tenant improvement allowance. Instead, I negotiated an option agreement within a two-year lease that gave me the right to purchase the building at a fixed price before the end of the lease period.

It was the early 1980s, and real estate values were severely depressed by mortgage interest rates that reached 18% at their peak. Condos were trending at the time, and builders were rolling them out like sod in response to a market hungry for lower-cost ownership alternatives. As I approached the option date, I applied for bank financing. My business was young, so banks approved only a portion of the purchase price.

There was no way I would walk away from the option. Interest rates had dropped to 12%, and the value of the building significantly appreciated beyond my option price. Then came the creative spark: if I could not afford the whole building, perhaps I could end up with most of it. Instead of pursuing second-source financing or partners, I decided to convert the building into condominiums and attempt to sell off some of the commercial units to existing tenants. Instead, I sold some residential units to a non-tenant buyer. At closing, I purchased the building, converted it, and conveyed a portion of it, all in a single waterfall closing event (a sequence in which ownership, financing, and sale transactions occur simultaneously). At the time, I thought of it as "desperation financing," but nothing fuels creative innovation quite like necessity.

In the chapters ahead, I outline the most common creative strategies you can deploy to revive deals where others fail. But do not stop at memorization. Your edge lies in discovering new applications of known tools. Become the agent who sees structure where others see dead ends.

Chapter 2:
Legal, Licensing & Brokerage Guidelines

Creative finance cannot succeed in the hands of professionals who ignore legal structure. In chapter 1, I established why creative deal-making matters, this chapter defines the boundaries. You must work within the confines of state law, licensing obligations, and brokerage policy or risk liability, suspension, or worse. Creativity without compliance is reckless.

Understand Your State's Laws

Real estate laws governing creative finance vary significantly by state. What is accepted in California may be scrutinized in Texas. In fact, Texas recently implemented restrictions on certain strategies in response to abuses, mostly by unlicensed actors. You cannot rely on hearsay from national webinars or investor meetups. As a licensed agent, you are bound to the statutes and case law of the jurisdiction in which you operate.

Begin by reviewing state-specific guidelines from your real estate commission or department. Understand how your state defines "equitable interest," whether it restricts wholesaling, and under what conditions seller financing triggers mortgage originator licensing laws. You are not expected to be a lawyer. But you are expected to know when to call one.

Brokerage Rules and Risk Management

Your broker carries the legal liability for your license. This fact governs everything. Creative strategies that seem exciting on paper may conflict with your brokerage's internal risk tolerance. Brokers must weigh errors and omissions (E&O) coverage, legal exposure, and company policy. You may find that certain deal types such as Subject-To or lease-options require preapproval or specialized documentation templates, or that they are outright prohibited by your brokerage.

Before structuring any non-standard deal, present it clearly to your broker. Demonstrate that you understand the mechanics, the disclosures, and the role you intend to play. Although your broker may require oversight for each transaction, you should endeavor to gain preapproval for the most common financing structures you intend to support so that you do not risk your credibility with clients or your brokerage. Broker alignment is not optional it is strategic protection.

Ethical Considerations and Disclosures

The Realtor Code of Ethics applies to all transactions, creative or conventional. That code demands honesty, full disclosure, and fair dealing, especially when clients do not fully understand the mechanics of a creative structure. Even when your client has significant buying and selling experience, you should treat them like first-time homebuyers when engaging in creative solutions. Be painstakingly careful to explain everything and test for understanding.

When using tools like seller carrybacks, lease-options, or wraparound mortgages, you must disclose the material facts, the risks involved, and who you represent. If you have any financial interest in the deal beyond a commission, disclose it in writing and obtain informed consent. I strongly urge you not to act as a principal in a transaction where you hold fiduciary relationship with another one of the parties.

Transactions such as "subject to" and others should always be presented with disclosures that fully explain potential risks. In most cases you will need to engage an attorney to prepare these for use in your transactions and in alignment with your state-specific requirements. Transparency protects everyone.

Licensing Boundaries and Roles

In creative deals, it is easy to blur the line between agent, investor, and advisor. That line must remain sharp. As a licensed agent, you may act as:

- A fiduciary representative for a buyer or seller.
- A principal in the transaction.
- A deal facilitator (with limitations depending on state laws).

You may not:

- Give legal advice.
- Collect fees outside of your licensed role without disclosure and brokerage approval.
- Present yourself as a neutral party when you have a stake in the outcome.

Protect your license by understanding your role and disclosing it clearly in writing to all parties to the transaction.

Who Not How

The title of coach Dan Sullivan's book, *Who Not How*, is both a question and a powerful statement. Most agents have their preferred escrow, title, and lender relationships, but your current posse may not have the skills or work within an environment that supports creative financing. You will likely need to level up your extended team to support your creative financing practice

If you must ask whether a lawyer should be involved, the answer is probably yes. Creative finance involves legal documents and unusual structures. You should never modify promissory notes, draft installment agreements, or advise clients on title strategies without legal oversight. Your job is not to replace the attorney, it is to recognize when one is needed. When it comes to all forms of seller finance you should assume that an attorney is always required.

Your first step is to assemble your team. First and foremost, you need an attorney partner who understands Subject-To transactions and can prepare the forms you need to augment your state-provided forms where they fall short. Your attorney may have to start from the ground up in some cases and for some states. You should always turn to your attorney to prepare every promissory note and security instrument for each transaction. Avoid using generic contract forms or security instrument templates provided by outside parties. These rarely meet the statutory requirements for your state let alone the additional complexities of a Subject-To transaction. Your specialized forms should be created by an attorney with state-specific real estate experience.

Next, you need to find a title company that is comfortable insuring Subject-To transactions. For non-attorney states your Escrow and Title services may be a single provider or separate. In either case, you need a strong working relationship with experienced professionals. Do not settle for less, particularly when you find yourself confronting a listing agent in a transaction who wants to work with their preferred title/escrow provider. If that provider does not have significant expertise, or is relying on someone else in their organization, remind the other agent that their license is on the line.

I strongly recommend that you find an attorney partner and competent escrow and title partners as a first step for preparing the foundation for your creative practice. Always delegate the drafting of promissory notes, deeds of trust, and mortgages to your attorney partner. Do not rely on title company attorneys for this. Title company attorneys represent the interests of the title insurer, not the client, and may be prohibited from offering legal advice to agents or consumers in some jurisdictions. Professional agents know their limits and guide clients toward protection.

In most states the first thing you will need to accomplish before you expand your business with creative financing strategies is to augment your forms library. Most states do not have the legal documents you need off the shelf. Ninety percent of the agents reading this book will need to develop a supplemental library working with your broker and an attorney with experience in creative deal structures. You need to assemble your team of professionals and establish your document augmentation before you put your toes into the water. Consider finding a mentor who is experienced in this space and is willing to teach you how to negotiate, underwrite, and manage these transactions. In this book I cover the how, you need to provide the who.

Dual Agency Conflicts in Creative Deals

Creative structures can compound the risks of dual agency. When a single agent represents both parties in a seller-financed or Subject-To transaction, the conflict is not just theoretical, it is structural.

> "I have never, nor will I ever engage in dual agency, and I urge you to do the same particularly when engaging in creative transaction management."

One party may be unsophisticated. The other may be a professional investor. Dual agency in this context can create disproportionate exposure. In all scenarios, thorough and ample disclosures are critical.

Brokerage Support vs. Resistance

Some brokerages resist creative finance out of fear, ignorance, or past litigation. Others embrace it and provide frameworks for risk-managed implementation.

If your broker is hesitant, do not attempt a "work around." Instead, educate them. Provide literature, case studies, or legal commentary that explains the transaction structure. Show how all parties can be protected and remain within legal bounds. If no is the answer, consider your options. Sometimes a yes can turn into a no. I had this happen to me with the first brokerage where I hung my license. I spent a lot of time educating my broker, but he got cold feet several months in. If this happens to you, move on because it is a clear indication that you're in the wrong place.

Marketing Compliance for Creative Terms

You must follow state and federal advertising laws when promoting creative terms. This includes compliance with:

- TILA (Truth in Lending Act) – governing how financing terms are presented.

- RESPA (Real Estate Settlement Procedures Act) – regulating kickbacks and disclosures.

Never advertise seller financing, lease-options, or assumable loans without first clearing the language with your broker and legal advisor. Avoid terms like "no banks needed" or "no credit check" unless you can fully substantiate them within legal parameters.

A safe approach: "Creative financing available. Terms subject to seller approval. Contact agent for details."

Final Note

This book does not offer legal advice. Always consult your broker and attorney when navigating creative strategies. Your role is not to have every answer but to know the right questions to protect your client and your license at every step.

Chapter 3:
The Four Levers of Creative Finance

Most agents define a "deal" by price and financing. Creative professionals, like you, see more. You understand that a transaction is an engineered structure, one that you can reshape, layer, or rebalance to solve problems that traditional deal structures do not address.

In this chapter I introduce a universal framework to evaluate and design creative transactions: **The Four Levers of Creative Finance**. When a deal is flexible, it is because the structure adapts across these four adjustable dimensions:

1. Control

2. Access to Capital

3. Risk Allocation and Mitigation

4. Terms

Together, these form the acronym **CART,** a simple way to remember the structural levers of creative finance. Consider it a control panel for moving deals forward. Each lever offers an opportunity to create value, solve problems, or unlock latent potential in a transaction. Mastery of these four elements transforms creative finance from improvisation into engineering.

What Makes a Deal "Creative"?

Creativity in real estate finance is not about being clever. It is about deploying structure with precision and intent. A deal earns the creative badge when it:

- Solves a problem that traditional financing cannot solve.

- Reconfigures control or obligation to produce mutual benefit.

- Reallocates risk or timeline in a way that unlocks value.

- Draws capital from unexpected sources while preserving compliance.

Creative does not mean recklessness. It means designed and purpose-built to overcome obstacles that price alone cannot fix.

Lever 1: Control

Creative finance often separates **control** from **ownership**. Options, lease-options, and equitable interests allow buyers or investors to control property decisions and benefit from appreciation without immediate title transfer. These instruments support:

- Renters building toward ownership.,

- Investors controlling properties with minimal capital.

- Sellers offloading management without sacrificing principal.

Control structures expand the pool of viable buyers and allow you to engage opportunities previously dismissed as unfinanceable by others. Think back to your license training courses. Control takes various forms in the construct of "estates." The many types of freehold and leasehold estates have new significance when you make the transition from working with typical deal structures to the world of creative solution engineering.

Scoring Guide
How to evaluate the use of the Control lever:

Score   Description

1   No separation of control and ownership. Buyer has no pre-closing authority.

2   Buyer has partial influence (e.g., lease), but no contractual right to direct property decisions.

3   Buyer holds an enforceable option or equitable interest. Moderate control over use or sale.

4   Full control through lease-option or wrap, may include resale rights or shared management.

5   Total engineered control: recorded option, assignability, resale authority, and profit participation.

Lever 2: Access to Capital

Traditional buyers go to banks. Creative professionals ask, "Who else could fund this?" Alternative capital structures include:

- Seller carrybacks, where equity becomes financing.
- Private lenders, often collateralized by real estate or business performance.
- Hypothecation, where a note from one deal funds another.
- Crowdfunding, fractional investments across many retail investors.
- Syndications, when investors pool resources.

The agent who understands capital flow becomes not just a transaction manager but a connector of resources and opportunity. Furthermore, these agents gain access to new types of buyers and sellers.

Scoring Guide
How to evaluate the use of the Access to Capital lever:

Score	Description
1	Buyer uses conventional bank financing exclusively.
2	Minor seller carryback or concessional funding; bank is still primary.
3	Seller-financed deal with no bank involvement. Straightforward structure.
4	Creative multi-source stack: seller carry plus private or hypothecated component.
5	Fully layered capital: multiple non-bank sources, hybrid structure, creative sequencing.

Lever 3: Risk Allocation and Mitigation

Every deal carries risk. The creative professional knows how to name it, measure it, and assign it.

Key elements include:

- Wraparound mortgages, which preserve underlying financing but shift servicing responsibility.

- Performance-based clauses, such as rent credits or milestone-based payments.

- Layered insurance, including non-payment guarantees or contingencies for repairs, vacancy, or default.

Creative structures are not about hiding risk they are about allocating it to the party best positioned to absorb it. These are just a few of the structures I introduce in this book, more will follow. The real creativity begins when you start combining them into hybrid models.

Scoring Guide
How to evaluate the use of the Risk Allocation lever:

Score	Description
1	No mitigation: Buyer absorbs all risks (default, repairs, vacancy, legal) without protections.
2	Basic protections: Inspection clause, title insurance, or seller disclosure only.
3	Moderate protection: Includes milestone-based clauses, repair escrows, or rental guarantees.
4	Multi-point strategy: Combines wraps, layered insurance, third-party servicing, or delayed close with contingencies.
5	Fully engineered: Allocation covers title risk, payment default, vacancy, and legal triggers (e.g., due-on-sale), using stacked instruments like performance insurance, collateral transfer clauses, and legal entity structuring.

Lever 4: Terms

Many agents focus on price. Creative professionals understand that terms define the deal. Creative financing expands your options using terms:

- Interest-only payments reduce monthly load while preserving equity.

- Deferred start dates or balloon notes can bridge capital timing gaps.

- Stepped amortization or graduated payments allow buyers to grow into the loan.

You can adjust terms to solve nearly any income-timing, affordability, or equity distribution challenge. And because every party values money differently over time, terms can often create a surplus value without changing price. One well-known creative financing expert, Pace Morby, often quips, "I can pay you any price you want provided you give me the right terms!"

Scoring Guide
How to evaluate the use of the Terms lever:

Score	Description
1	Standard amortized loan with fixed monthly payments.
2	Slight deviation (e.g., balloon or interest-only) without broader customization.
3	Simple flexible term (e.g., deferred start or adjustable rate).

4   Layered solution: stepped payments, graduated interest, or customized schedules.

5   Advanced term stack: multi-tiered instruments, payoff windows, equity-sharing, or performance-based amortization.

Example: Subject-To with Seller Carry Hybrid

Deal Summary: Buyer takes title via subject-to acquisition of an existing mortgage. Seller remains liable for the loan but is protected through a mirror wrap. (a mirror wrap is a note and all-inclusive deed of trust or mortgage that mirrors the current terms of the existing note) Seller provides a secondary note as carryback financing. The buyer contributes cash to cover all closing costs for both parties.

CART Evaluation: Subject-To Hybrid

Lever	Score	Rationale
Control	5	Buyer receives full title and controls disposition, resale, and management. Wrap structure reinforces control while protecting seller.
Access to Capital	5	No new bank loan is required. Capital stack includes subject-to existing loan, seller carry, and buyer-paid closing. Highly leveraged with minimal cash outlay.
Risk Allocation and Mitigation	3	Seller is protected via mirror wrap, but due-on-sale risk remains.

Terms	4	Carryback note introduces flexibility. However, structure lacks complex amortization or income-matching provisions that would elevate to a 5.

Total Score: 17 / 20

Note: This structure showcases how you can use multiple levers to create a robust, transaction. Areas for enhancement include risk protection depth and more advanced term structuring.

Example: Lease-Option with Rent Credit and Deferred Closing

Deal Summary: Buyer enters into a lease-option agreement with a two-year term. A portion of the monthly rent is credited toward the purchase. The title does not transfer until the option is exercised. Buyer has the right to assign the option. Seller agrees to fixed purchase price but defers closing, allowing buyer time to improve credit and qualify for traditional financing.

CART Evaluation: Lease Option

Lever	Score	Rationale
Control	4	Buyer holds assignable option and directs use of property but does not yet hold title or full authority.
Access to Capital	3	Buyer is leveraging monthly rent toward equity but does not have external capital layering. No seller carry or external financing involved.

| Risk Allocation and Mitigation | 4 | Deferred closing and rent credit create milestone-based risk control. Buyer may exit if conditions change. The seller maintains ownership until the buyer performs. |
| Terms | 5 | Terms are intentionally designed: rent credits, deferred closing, fixed strike price, and flexible assignment make this a fully engineered timeline. |

Total Score: 16 / 20

> ⚠ This is a classic affordability bridge structure, suitable for buyers with unstable credit or cash flow. Risk is reasonably balanced, and the buyer gains leveraged access without requiring immediate financing.

Conclusion

Creative finance is not a set of tricks. It is a discipline rooted in systems thinking. By mastering control, access to capital, risk, and terms, you can:

- Solve complex client problems,
- Expand your market influence,
- Close deals others cannot even see and attract more clients

Every creative deal is different. But every creative deal is driven by these four levers. Each lever score reflects the degree of strategic leverage and creative advantage to the structuring party, which is typically the buyer or representing agent. High scores indicate sophisticated deal design, not necessarily mutual fairness. I encourage all creative practitioners to balance innovation with disclosure, ethics, and long-term relationship equity.

Chapter 4:
Seller Financing Fundamentals

Seller financing remains the most versatile and field-proven instrument in creative real estate finance. It is the first strategy in this handbook that fully activates the four levers that I introduced in the previous chapter.

Introduction: Seller Financing Through the Four Levers

This structure-centered approach allows you to reposition deals that would otherwise fail under conventional underwriting. With seller financing, you do not merely facilitate a transaction, you architect an outcome.

Seller financing enables:

- Immediate structuring flexibility without third-party interference.
- Customizable terms that reflect mutual goals.
- Deployment of seller equity as deal capital.
- Improved control and fallback remedies for both parties.

Next, I evaluate the mechanics and application of seller financing through the lens of each CART lever.

Security Instruments: Mortgage vs. Deed of Trust

You secure seller-financed transactions by recording a mortgage or a deed of trust. These legal instruments govern foreclosure remedies, timeline enforcement, and party relationships. Your state statutes determine which is used.

Aspect	Mortgage	Deed of Trust
Parties Involved	Two: Borrower and Lender	Three: Borrower, Lender (Beneficiary), Trustee
Security Role	Secures loan with lien on property	Secures loan with lien, but through trustee
Foreclosure Type	Typically, judicial	Typically, administrative
Timeline for Foreclosure	Often protracted (months to years)	Often expedited (30–90 days typical)
Power of Sale Clause	Optional	Standard

⚠️ See Appendix in the book download for detailed state-by-state application.

Structural Variants of Seller Financing

Each structure below includes a formal CART evaluation using a 1–5 scale. The total score reflects design flexibility and creative leverage not simplicity or safety. High scores indicate strategic range, but do not indicate suitability for all clients.

Simple Seller Carryback

Description: Buyer makes a downpayment that may be less than conventional lender requirements, and the seller conveys full title and carries a note secured by a first-position deed of trust or mortgage. This is the cleanest application when the property is free and clear.

CART Evaluation: Seller Carryback

Lever	Score	Rationale
Control	5	Buyer holds legal title and disposition authority.
Access to Capital	3	Seller funds the balance in lieu of bank.
Risk	3	Moderate; foreclosure options are clear.
Terms	3	Customizable but often kept simple.
Total Score	14 / 20	Efficient, straightforward structure.

This structure is ideal for sellers who want to defer capital gains and want consistent income without rental management responsibilities, such as "tired landlords." Investors who seek to hold numerous properties benefit because while there is not a legal limit to the number of mortgages one person can have, in practice, most lenders, especially those offering conventional loans, typically limit the number to no more than 10. Seller carryback is ideal for buyers who may not be able to qualify with a conventional lender or might need a lower interest rate or downpayment. If you are working with a seller who is stuck on a price above market value, you can meet their price by balancing that with favorable terms for the buyer, creating a win-win for both parties.

Cautions: Make sure that your Escrow/title company is comfortable and competent to provide the promissory note and security instruments. Consider using an attorney to draft these. Better still, use an attorney.

Land Contract / Contract for Deed / Installment Sale

Description: Buyer takes equitable title and possession; seller retains legal title until fulfillment. Title transfer occurs upon final payment.

CART Evaluation: Installment Sales

Lever	Score	Rationale
Control	3	Buyer controls use but lacks full ownership rights.
Access to Capital	4	Bypasses institutional financing.
Risk	3	Varies by state; forfeiture laws may apply.
Terms	4	Highly flexible across timelines and rates.

Total Score: 14 / 20 Effective structure with mid-range leverage.

Benefits: Because only the security instrument distinguishes this from simple seller carryback, the benefits of land contracts are virtually the same as for seller carryback above. You may have an easier time convincing a seller to work with this structure because they may feel more secure by retaining actual title until they are paid in full. You should thoroughly discuss the nuances of actual and equitable title with your seller.

Cautions: You must be familiar with your state's regulatory treatment of these, which can vary widely state-to-state. You must educate yourself on the property forfeiture laws in your state. These are often very different for land contracts than for standard foreclosures. You must also understand how to secure the buyer's interest in the property through public recording. Be certain to inform your buyer or seller of all associated risks so that they can make an informed decision. Include exit provisions for the buyer such as a right to refinance out. Consider adding provisions that prevent or limit the seller's ability to add encumbrances. If you are representing a buyer in a transaction like this, be certain to identify and disclose any underlying financing or other liens on the property.

Access the book download for an appendix on recording requirements and remedies by state.

All-Inclusive Trust Deed (AITD) / Wrap

Description: The seller benefits from creating a new note that wraps around their existing mortgage, embedding the remaining portion of the underlying loan balance with or without additional equity from the seller into a higher-value higher interest rate note that generates a spread income for the seller.

This structure maximizes both the value of the seller's property and monetizes the value of the underlying financing. By keeping the loan in place, the seller retains access to equity. This benefits buyers who may not be able to qualify with a conventional lender or might need a lower interest rate or downpayment. Title transfers to the buyer.

Do not structure AITDs casually. The due-on-sale exposure must be fully disclosed and the responsibility for the costs associated with the defense loan acceleration should be assigned to the seller in the contract. You might ask why? I have a rule of thumb that the party who benefits most from the transaction should be responsible for defending it. I also recommend that you always follow the best practice of using an experienced attorney to prepare the note and security instruments for these.

CART Evaluation: Wraps

Lever	Score	Rationale
Control	5	Buyer gains title; seller may embed override clauses.
Access to Capital	5	Leverages existing mortgage without new loan.
Risk	3	Due-on-sale remains active
Terms	4	Amortization, balloon, and interest can all be tailored.

Total Score: 17 / 20 High-leverage structure for experienced parties.

Subject-To

A Subject-To transaction occurs when the buyer takes title to the property while the seller's existing mortgage remains in place. The loan stays in the seller's name, but the buyer assumes responsibility for making payments. The lender is not formally notified, and no new financing is required. This strategy is often used when the seller's existing mortgage has a favorable interest rate that the buyer wishes to preserve.

This strategy enables buyers to acquire property without obtaining new financing. The buyer often steps into a loan with a below-market rate and avoids traditional underwriting requirements. This may also provide an exit for sellers in default or at risk of foreclosure. Subject-To deals are particularly powerful in high-interest environments when legacy financing becomes an asset in itself. For the right seller, this structure can eliminate holding costs, avert damage to credit, and offload a property in distress.

Due-on-sale clauses are active in nearly every modern deed of trust or mortgage. This means that the lender has the right, not the obligation, to call the note due when title transfers without their consent. You must fully disclose this to all parties. The seller's interest must be secured using a mirror wrap or similar protective instrument, and legal counsel should always prepare these documents. Assign the cost and responsibility for defending against loan acceleration contractually; ideally to the party who benefits most. Never mislead any party into thinking the lender approved of this structure unless you have written confirmation.

CART Evaluation: Subject-To

Lever	Score	Rationale
Control	5	Buyer receives title and full management rights.
Access to Capital	5	No new financing; buyer steps into existing mortgage.
Risk	2	Due-on-sale and seller exposure unless mitigated by wrap.
Terms	4	Allows flexible layering via carry, balloon, or deferred pay.

Total Score: 16 / 20 High leverage; success hinges on disclosure and protection.

Performance Mortgages / Second-Position Carries

A performance mortgage is a second-position security instrument held by the seller that ties repayment obligations to defined buyer outcomes. Unlike a conventional second mortgage, which follows a fixed amortization schedule, a performance mortgage includes event-driven triggers such as:

- Resale or refinance of the property.

- Completion of a renovation project.

- Achievement of lease-up targets or income milestones.

For instance, a seller might structure repayment to begin only after the buyer completes a multi-unit rehab and reaches 90% occupancy.

This tool allows a seller to remain financially involved in the deal while aligning repayment with buyer execution. It is especially valuable in subject-to transactions, partial seller carrybacks, or deals where the buyer's ability or obligation to perform matures over time. These are excellent fits for deals requiring graduated incentives or layered financing. The seller retains a secured interest in the property's upside or operational success. Performance mortgages often include default clauses that convert the obligation to an immediate due balance upon missed benchmarks, giving the seller legal standing and structured recourse.

When you add performance measures to a promissory note it is essential to avoid ambiguity that can lead to confusion or disputes. I recommend always using an attorney with appropriate experience to draft these.

Sidebar: What About Bridge Loans?

Bridge loans are short-term, interest-only loans designed to fund a purchase while another asset is liquidated. While typically offered by private lenders, sellers may replicate this model by issuing short-term, event-driven second-position notes. These "seller-originated bridges" enable strategic flexibility offering liquidity in exchange for higher yield and a secured stake in the property's timeline. Unlike private bridge loans, seller-originated versions are not subject to the same underwriting requirements but may still trigger disclosure obligations depending on jurisdiction.

CART Evaluation: Performance Mortgage

Lever	Score	Rationale
Control	3	Buyer retains possession; seller holds event-based leverage.
Access to Capital	4	Adds non-bank capital layer without disturbing senior lien.
Risk	4	Seller protection improves with performance clauses.
Terms	5	Highly engineered structures adaptable to outcomes.

Total Score 16 / 20 Strong tool for partial equity retention and risk mitigation.

Compliance: Legal and Regulatory Overlays

Compliance is not only a legal imperative but also a trust-building advantage that distinguishes you as a professional solutions provider. You must be aware of both federal and state laws governing seller financing. While federal regulations provide exceptions or relaxed rules for sellers that engage in three or less transactions in a calendar year, state-specific rules may be more restrictive. I provide examples of some state overlays, but you must educate yourself on state law and understand your brokerage-specific restrictions, if they apply.

Federal Regulations Governing Seller Financing

Several federal laws and regulations apply to seller-financed real estate transactions, particularly when the buyer intends to use the property as a primary residence:

- **Truth in Lending Act (TILA) and Regulation Z**: TILA mandates clear disclosure of loan terms, including the annual percentage rate (APR), total finance charges, and payment schedules. Regulation Z implements TILA's provisions, ensuring transparency in lending practices.

- **Dodd-Frank's Three-Property Rule:** Under the Dodd-Frank Act, a seller (individual, trust, estate, or entity) who finances the sale of three or fewer residential properties in a 12-month period may qualify for an exemption from certain federal requirements, including the need to be licensed as a mortgage loan originator. To qualify for this exemption, the following conditions must be met:

- **Property Ownership:** The seller must own each property they finance.

- **Construction:** The seller must not have constructed or acted as a contractor for the construction of the residence in the ordinary course of business

Loan Terms:

- **Fully Amortizing:** The financing must be fully amortizing; balloon payments are not permitted.

- **Interest Rate:** The loan must have a fixed interest rate or an adjustable rate that resets after five or more years, with reasonable annual and lifetime limits on interest rate increases.

- **Ability to Repay:** The seller must determine, in good faith, that the buyer has a reasonable ability to repay the loan. You should consider using a registered mortgage loan originator to qualify the buyer to provide your seller with defensibility and objectivity.

It is important to note that these exemptions apply only to seller-financed transactions involving residential properties of one to four units where the buyer intends to occupy the property as their primary residence.

- Secure and Fair Enforcement for Mortgage Licensing Act (SAFE Act): This act requires individuals engaged in the business of mortgage loan origination to be licensed and registered, aiming to enhance consumer protection and reduce fraud.

State-Level Restrictions Exceeding Federal Standards

While federal laws provide a baseline, individual states may impose additional regulations on seller financing:

- **Licensing and Registration**: Some states require seller-financers to obtain a mortgage broker or lender license, even if they only engage in a few transactions per year.

- **Contract Requirements**: States may mandate specific contract terms, disclosures, or formatting to ensure clarity and fairness in seller-financed agreements. These may be both state-specific and transaction-type-specific.

- **Consumer Protections**: Enhanced protections, such as mandatory cooling-off periods or restrictions on balloon payments, may be enforced to safeguard buyers at the state level.

Given the variability in state laws, it's crucial for parties involved in seller financing to consult local regulations or seek legal counsel to ensure compliance. The following are some specific state examples:

Texas

In Texas, individuals providing seller financing for residential properties must comply with the state's version of the SAFE Act. This includes obtaining a Residential Mortgage Loan Originator (RMLO) license unless they qualify for specific exemptions, such as financing only one property in a 12-month period. The Texas Department of Savings and Mortgage Lending oversees these licensing requirements.

Washington State

Washington enforces enhanced consumer protection measures for seller-financed transactions. For example, the state requires that sellers assess the buyer's ability to repay the loan, like the federal *Ability-to-Repay* rule, but with additional state-specific criteria. Furthermore, Washington law provides buyers with extended foreclosure timelines, and mandates clear disclosure of all loan terms to prevent predatory lending practices

Minnesota

In Minnesota, seller-financed contracts must include a statutory cancellation notice, giving buyers a 60-day period to cure defaults before the seller can terminate the contract. This provision offers greater protection than the federal standard, which does not specify a notice period. Additionally, Minnesota law prohibits certain balloon payment structures in seller-financed deals to prevent sudden large payments that buyers may be unable to afford.

California

Seller financing is permitted, but sellers must adhere to both federal and state regulations. While California does not have a specific statute governing seller financing, general real estate and lending laws apply. You should ensure that contracts are properly drafted and deliver all applicable disclosures.

Misconceptions and Structural Clarity

Myth: Seller must own the property outright. Wraps, AITDs, and second-position notes allow encumbered properties to be financed creatively.

Wraps do not eliminate the underlying liens they structure around them. This allows title transfer while the original loan remains active, typically secured by a mirror note or override clause.

Myth: Only low-credit buyers use seller financing. Clarification: Professionals, Investors, self-employed buyers, and foreign nationals often seek speed and privacy not leniency.

Conclusion: Seller Financing as Structural Leverage

Seller financing is not a workaround. It is a structure capable of bending each of the Four Levers to align needs, solve problems, and close deals that conventional lenders decline. When deployed correctly, it:

- Unlocks equity as capital.

- Transfers control without delay.

- Redistributes and contains risk.

- Reshapes terms to create affordability and appeal.

When you master creative financing techniques, you become more than a sales agent. You elevate yourself to a solutions architect. This is how elite agents stay indispensable in a market where automation outpaces tradition.

Chapter 5:
Subject-To Transactions

Subject-To transactions are not merely a tactic; they are a high-leverage tool in the creative finance arsenal. In an environment where interest rates have doubled or tripled from historical lows, the ability to preserve existing mortgage terms can determine whether a deal is financially viable. In this chapter I explain the mechanics, ethics, and applications of Subject-To structures with the clarity and rigor required by licensed professionals.

Why Subject-To?

When you structure these properly and provide complete disclosers, a Subject-To arrangement allows a buyer to acquire property by taking over the existing mortgage payments without formally assuming the loan. Not only does this provide the buyer with access to better interest rates, but it often provides faster amortization depending on the loan's maturity.

These transactions also benefit sellers. Consider the case of an active-duty couple who purchased their home at the height of the market frenzy in 2021 and a few years later found themselves in the middle of a soft market with redeployment orders that take them overseas for three years. I was able to attract an investor buyer who stepped up to a higher purchase price to realize the savings on the cost of money.

This type of transaction can benefit sellers facing foreclosure. Rather than wearing the scarlet letter of foreclosure or short sale on their credit report for seven years, a Subject-To transaction that reverts the note to a steady performing state can enable a debtor to rebuild their credit in as little as three years if they then practice good credit hygiene.

Subject-To is particularly effective when:

- The seller faces foreclosure or hardship.

- The mortgage has a significantly below-market interest rate.

- The buyer lacks access to conventional lending but can perform.

- The seller wants to avoid further liability and offload the asset.

Mechanics of a Subject-To Transaction

In a Subject-To deal, the buyer takes legal title to the property while the seller's existing mortgage remains in place. The loan stays in the seller's name; however, the buyer assumes the obligation of making the monthly payments. The original lender is not notified, and the transaction is not contingent upon the buyer qualifying for new financing.

Key components include:

- Title transfers to the buyer at closing.

- Seller's mortgage remains recorded against the property.

- Buyer takes over payments, often through a third-party servicer.

- Insurance policies and taxes must be updated to reflect the new ownership while maintaining lender protections.

This structure is often mischaracterized as an assumption, but the distinction is critical: in a formal assumption, the lender approves and replaces the borrower. In Subject-To, the lender remains unaware unless triggered by external events. It is not appropriate for every scenario. Subject-To is a tool of precision, not desperation.

Contractual and Ethical Boundaries

Every Subject-To transaction contains an inherent contractual tension: the due-on-sale clause. Virtually all modern mortgages include language granting the lender the right, but not the obligation to call the loan due if the property transfers without the lender's consent. The clause is real. The probability of enforcement varies widely depending on lender policy, borrower performance, and public record visibility. It is important that you understand that this is a contractual breach only and that this action does not constitute fraud.

The Garn-St. Germain Depository Institutions Act of 1982 is a U.S. federal law that was primarily aimed at helping savings and loan institutions during the financial crisis in the early 1980s. The Act allows lenders to enforce due-on-sale clauses in mortgage contracts. This means if a homeowner sells or transfers their property, the lender can demand full repayment of the loan with exceptions, particularly for transfers into a living trust or transfers between family members under certain conditions.

Key Exceptions for Family Transfers

According to **12 U.S.C. § 1701j-3(d)**, lenders cannot enforce the due-on-sale clause in the following family-related scenarios:

1. **Inheritance by Relatives**: If a borrower passes away and the property is transferred to a relative through a will, intestate succession, or operation of law, the lender cannot demand immediate repayment of the mortgage. This provision ensures that heirs can continue making mortgage payments without refinancing, even if they might not qualify for a new loan.

2. **Transfer to Spouse or Children**: A borrower can transfer ownership of the property to their spouse or children during their lifetime without activating the due-on-sale clause. This includes full ownership transfers or adding them as joint owners.

3. **Transfers Following Divorce or Legal Separation**: If, as part of a divorce decree, legal separation agreement, or property settlement, the borrower's spouse becomes the owner of the property, the due-on-sale clause cannot be enforced.

4. **Transfer into an Inter Vivos Trust**: Transferring the property into a living (inter vivos) trust, where the borrower remains a beneficiary and continues to occupy the property, does not

trigger the due-on-sale clause. This facilitates estate planning by allowing property to be placed in a trust without necessitating mortgage repayment.

Pursuant to the Living Trust exception, some investors use land trusts to obscure public visibility of title transfer. While this may reduce the risk of triggering the due-on-sale clause, it should not be used to deceive any party. Therin lies the rub. Fractured Shakespeare quotes and tangled webs notwithstanding, what purpose does this serve if not to deceive?

As a real estate professional, your ethical responsibilities demand that you:

- Protect all parties in the transaction.

- Disclose the existence and implications of the due-on-sale clause to both parties.

- Avoid implying lender approval without written confirmation.

- Recommend legal review of all documentation.

- Abstain from acting as both principal and agent even if it is legally permissible.

Transparency is not optional. Informed consent must be written, acknowledged, and retained.

I once found myself embroiled in a heated argument with a broker regarding Subject-To. He was insisting that Subject-To is illegal. After breaking through the argument by showing him that **Loans taken subject to** is a line item on both sides of the ledger on the HUD-1 form as shown in Figure 5-1, and that it was a checkbox in the financing section of some of our state's purchase agreements, he switched into decrying it as a moral issue. It was abundantly clear that we were not going to reach détente.

J. Summary of Borrower's Transaction		K. Summary of Seller's Transaction	
100. Gross Amount Due from Borrower		**400. Gross Amount Due to Seller**	
101. Contract sales price		401. Contract sales price	
102. Personal property		402. Personal property	
103. Settlement charges to borrower (line 1400)		403.	
104.		404.	
105.		405.	
Adjustment for items paid by seller in advance		Adjustment for items paid by seller in advance	
106. City/town taxes to		406. City/town taxes to	
107. County taxes to		407. County taxes to	
108. Assessments to		408. Assessments to	
109.		409.	
110.		410.	
111.		411.	
112.		412.	
120. Gross Amount Due from Borrower		**420. Gross Amount Due to Seller**	
200. Amount Paid by or in Behalf of Borrower		**500. Reductions in Amount Due to seller**	
201. Deposit or earnest money		501. Excess deposit (see instructions)	
202. Principal amount of new loan(s)		502. Settlement charges to seller (line 1400)	
203. Existing loan(s) taken subject to		503. Existing loan(s) taken subject to	
204.		504. Payoff of first mortgage loan	
205.		505. Payoff of second mortgage loan	

Figure 5-1: Excerpt from the HUD-1 form showing line items
for Existing loan(s) taken subject to on both sides of the transaction.

Risk Mitigation

The most powerful risk mitigation strategy when approaching a Subject-To transaction is to avoid engaging with loans that have a higher risk of a lender noticing the transaction. Loans originated by lenders that also service their own portfolios are at higher risk of scrutiny. These include loans issued by small community banks, family-owned banks, credit unions, and other lenders that originate and service their own portfolios.

Prior to engaging in a Subject-To transaction you must investigate each loan by using your title-company-provided property profiling service or other data service to pull the deed(s) of trust or recorded mortgage instrument(s). If there are multiple loans on the property, you must examine each one. I always create a folio and download copies of all available security instruments to inform my underwriting process.

When a Home Equity Line of Credit (HELOC) is involved, there are additional considerations and risks. First, these tend to be issued by smaller lenders like credit unions and therefore almost always have a higher associated risk, however there are larger lenders that issue these, and you will find some that are packaged and sold into the secondary market. Keep in mind that HELOCs bear variable interest rates that are tied to a benchmark such as prime or LIBOR making it impossible to predict the payments. If the draw period of the HELOC is still open, it is possible for the borrower/seller to draw on any available credit. You should have the seller work with the HELOC lender to close the draw period if possible.

Most loans originated by large lenders are destined for the secondary markets where they are bundled and securitized with other loans. The best indication of this is the indicia for Mortgage Electronic Registration Systems, Inc. (MERS). MERS functions as a nominee and provides a single source for tracking beneficiaries and servicing rights.

Founded in 1995, MERS was created by a consortium of major mortgage lenders, Fannie Mae, Freddie Mac, and the Mortgage Bankers Association to modernize and digitize the mortgage recording system, which was previously fragmented, and paper based. It eliminates the need to record assignments of mortgages in county land records. You can purchase a subscription to the MERS database, which at the time of this writing was $250.00 per year.

See the Appendix in the book download for state-by-state treatment of MERS in the foreclosure process.

You can identify these loans because the MERS registration is easy to spot as you can see in Figure 5-2.

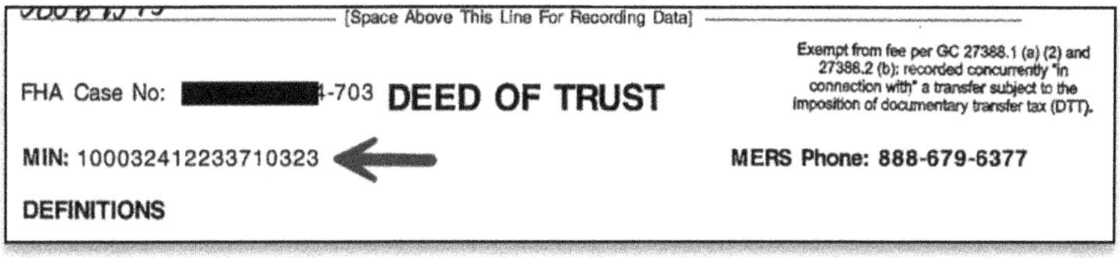

Figure 5-2: Header from a deed of trust shows the MERS Identification Number (MIN) opposite the MERS phone number. MERS is further identified in the "Parties" section.

Negotiating a Subject-To Purchase

The seller's cash at closing typically anchors the negotiations for most Subject-To transactions. Once you satisfy the seller's cash requirement or "equity out," you calculate the purchase price by adding to that, the remaining balance of the loan(s) and other liens for which you are taking responsibility. When you are dealing with significant arrears or when loans are defaulted and in pre-foreclosure, there may be zero or negative equity in the property so the cash out in these cases is better characterized as moving money.

With defaulted loans, the process is further complicated by the need to obtain reinstatement letters to capture all costs associated with the transaction. Some investors are eager to get a property under contract and will gladly use estimated numbers. I prefer to slow the roll enough to execute the research necessary to fully underwrite the transaction to produce an accurate purchase agreement rather than amending and adding terms. Your escrow officer will thank you for this!

It is important to indicate which party is responsible for the cost of defending a loan acceleration (due-on-sale) in your contract. I believe that this burden belongs to the party who benefits most from the arrangement, typically the buyer. When a seller initiates the effort to sell using this method, the seller should be the party responsible for defending an acceleration. You should also have a contractual clause that specifies how the parties will respond to an acceleration such as reverting to a land contract or installment sale.

Underwriting a Subject-To Transaction

Underwriting is the process you engage to determine the correct numbers to use in the purchase agreement, promissory note, and wrap-around mortgage. During this process you also vet the deal by uncovering undisclosed encumbrances that might kill it. The first step toward underwriting a Subject-To deal is information gathering.

You need to pull all active or potentially active deeds of trust on the title. You need a current statement for each loan that you are considering for inclusion in the transaction and if the seller can produce it, a copy of the original promissory note is very helpful, especially if you find a discrepancy when you run an amortization in the next step. If there is a current delinquency or a history of delinquencies such as multiple Notices of Default (NOD) or Notice of Sale (NOS), you should look for evidence of loan modifications. These typically manifest on title as additional deeds of trust or mortgages and may or may not be interest bearing or have payments associated with them. Sellers who have had loan modifications are often unaware that they result in additional liens. Give them the benefit of the doubt rather than assuming that they are withholding information and remember that you need to be thorough in your investigation for this reason.

For each amortizing loan you need to run an amortization schedule. You use the loan amortization to determine the correct principal balance close of escrow to true up your purchase price. This also provides the details required for your attorney to draft the new promissory note and wrap-around mortgage.

After running your amortization schedule, compare the principal balance shown on the current statement to the scheduled principal balance on the amortization. If these agree viola, your job is easy. If they are off by a small amount, say less than $30.00, you can either ignore this or jigger your amortization a little to get the two into agreement. Sometimes you will run into these small discrepancies that are inexplicable. These might simply be the result of variances in the amortization calculator you are using versus the one the lender used, or it might be that there were small adjustments made to the principal amount before closing that are not reflected in the recorded instruments. This is where a copy of the original promissory note might shed light on the source.

If you find a large discrepancy your next move is to look for an explanation. Know that you may not be able to find an audit trail to follow so you need to decide how much time you want to spend in the proverbial rabbit hole. For instance, the way lenders implement forbearance periods does not always produce an audit trail. They are handled through billing cycles rather than loan modifications. In these cases, you will need to work from the statement and start an amortization based on the current principal amount and date and run it for the remaining months in the loan duration.

Now that you have the loan(s) quantified, you must identify all other liens on the property and determine how you will handle them. Leased items such as SOLAR, water conditioning, and security systems are generally easy to transfer and do not impact on the sale price. Note that you can also keep paying for these without a formal assumption, but these types of obligations are best transferred.

For loans that are in default and are approaching an auction date, besides postponing any imminent sale to ensure that you have enough time to reinstate it, you need to request a reinstatement letter from the lender. The reinstatement amount will include penalties, additional interest, and additional lender fees.

Calculating the Sale Price

Performing Loans: Price = Seller Cash + Loan Balances

**Non-performing   Price = Seller Cash+ Loan Balances + Arrears +
Loans:**   Fees

⚠ Real estate transfer taxes are handled differently across the states that have them. In California and Georgia, for instance, transfer tax is calculated on the difference between the sale price and liens that the buyer assumes. On the other hand, Florida charges transfer taxes on the total sale price. Make sure that you familiarize yourself with the mechanics of transfer taxes, both state and local, in your practice area.

Securing the Seller's Interest

Because the loan remains in the seller's name it is your ultimate objective to protect their interest by securing it using a promissory note and an All-Inclusive Deed of Trust (AIDT) or wraparound mortgage. This preserves the seller's right to foreclose on the Subject-To buyer if the buyer stops paying the loan. Many investors and escrow agents execute Subject-To transactions without securing the seller. These "naked Subject-To" transactions create additional risk for the seller. Although the purchase agreement probably states or implies that the buyer is responsible for the loan payments going forward, it lacks the specifics of an accurate promissory note and the teeth of a security instrument.

A comprehensive promissory note should reflect an accurate start date, number of payments, and the amount of each payment excluding tax and insurance impounds. Normally, the payments "mirror" the underlying loan and cover the period from close of escrow until the loan is paid.

Another name for this is a "mirror wrap." You can also introduce additional terms such as a balloon payment that terminates the note prior to maturity requiring the buyer to sell or refinance the loan prior to the balloon date. If you are dealing with a sale to an end buyer rather than an investor, be certain to review current seller financing rules for your state before introducing a balloon payment.

Some investors acquire properties using the Subject-To method for the purpose of reselling the property using a wraparound mortgage to create cashflow by arbitraging the interest rate. This advanced strategy requires significant cash or fungible reserves to cover carry costs, defaults, and foreclosures to protect the credit of the original borrower.

Using a third-party servicing company to service the new note can provide a sense of comfort to the seller in a Subject-To transaction. The servicing company will process the payments as an intermediary and keep the seller informed of the payments and proactively alert the seller if the buyer misses a payment. Because this introduces an additional point of failure (potential delay), I recommend that the buyer remain one payment ahead to prevent late payments due to processing delays.

The alternative to using a third-party is logon sharing. The buyer and seller are entering a long-term relationship. If they can share a loan, they can also share a logon if necessary. In most cases it is possible to add users to the loan portal. The only time this becomes a challenge is when the loan uses the same account as the seller's banking. In this case it may be possible to separate the two. I always make a point to introduce the buyer and seller at a closing conference to review the rules of the relationship and to make certain they have each other's contact information and understand the importance of their ongoing cooperation.

Elements of the Contract

I always recommend using state provided standardized contracts for all real estate transactions as these are most recognizable to broker and agents, escrow officers, attorneys and other real estate professionals. Unfortunately, none of the state form sets I have reviewed handle a Subject-To transaction completely. By far, California has the best coverage, and Arizona is a close second. Neither state thoroughly addresses the requirements.

At a high level you need a purchase agreement, a seller financing addendum with provisions for Subject-To transactions, and a set of disclosures and acknowledgements. No matter what your state provides, you will need to augment it. For California, I engaged an attorney to create the disclosures and acknowledgements, which we have signed along with the contract and again at time of signing for closing as additional assurance.

The body of the purchase agreement should have a place to note the loan(s) to be taken subject-to indicating that these are subject-to loans. The amount stated in the purchase agreement is the expected principal balance at closing, not the original amount of the loan. In most cases a Subject-To transaction does not have financing or appraisal contingencies, however a buyer might add one as a matter of due diligence.

The next specialized contract document you need is a seller financing addendum. Of the dozen states I explored, only California has provisions for characterizing one or more senior encumbrances for a Subject-To transaction as well as provisions for a seller carry. Many Subject-To contracts are hybrids containing both one or more senior loans and a seller carryback. Seller financing addendums in states that do have these, accommodate seller carryback only.

Conclusion: A Tool Not a Shortcut

Subject-To is not a workaround for unqualified buyers. It is a strategic design for aligning opportunity with affordability, when used ethically and with legal diligence. Your credibility as a real estate professional depends on your ability to structure, disclose, and protect all parties. This chapter equips you to do exactly that.

Chapter 6:
Wraparound Mortgages

Wraparound mortgages, or "wraps," are a high-functioning tool in the creative finance repertoire. They allow investors to monetize existing financing while creating positive outcomes for buyers and themselves. In this chapter I define the structure, evaluate the risks, and guide you in navigating wrap transactions.

Why Wraparound Mortgages?

In Chapter 5 you learned about using a wraparound mortgage (mirror wrap) to protect the seller in a Subject-To transaction. In this chapter I explain wraparound mortgages or all-inclusive deeds of trust for profit. By employing this exit strategy an investor generates positive cashflow by arbitraging the interest rate, or by selling for a higher price, or both. They acquire Subject-To deals for the purpose of selling on a wrap.

In this chapter I focus on wraps promulgated by investors acting as intermediary buyers who then resell using a wrap, but it is important to note that this strategy can work for savvy sellers as well. If you have a seller who owns a home with a good interest rate and is having a difficult time selling their home, wrapping their own loan might be the key to attracting a buyer.

Investor benefits:

- Creates recurring monthly profit.

- High leverage with minimal cash required.

- Eliminates overhead associated with rental properties.

End buyer benefits:

- Acquire property without qualifying for new financing.

- Potentially lower interest rates.

- Lower cash requirements.

Mechanics of a Wrap

Unless the seller is wrapping their own loan, selling real estate on a wrap involves two transactions. The first is a Subject-To transaction (A to B) and the second is the sale to the end-byer (B to C) The end buyer makes payments to the seller or investor based on the new, typically higher balance, while the seller continues to pay their original mortgage or the mortgage that they acquired subject-to. Alternatively, the seller or investor arranges for a note servicing company to service the new note. The servicing company then distributes the payments to the original lender and the seller holding the wrap note. The result is a single-payment system that embeds the original debt into a new, inclusive note that produces investor yield as illustrated in Figure 6-1

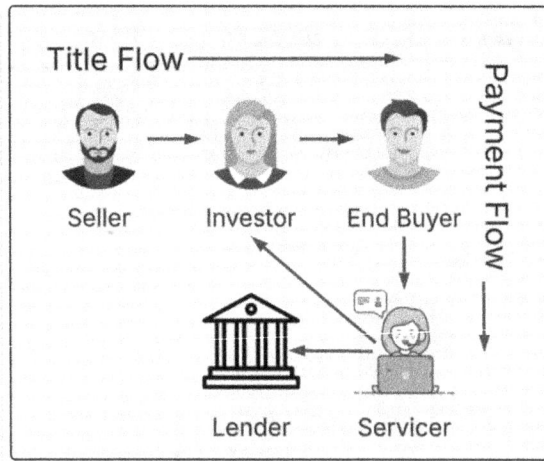

Figure 6-1: Wrap title and payment flow.

Like a Subject-To transaction, the end buyer takes title to the home, but there are ultimately two buyers; the investor buyer and the homestead buyer who will occupy the home as a primary resident. Although some investors are savvy enough to have a buyer waiting in the wings, these transactions typically have a holding period for the investor while they market the property for resale. This requires significant financial resources for carrying costs should the timeline for the sale stretch beyond planned or should acts of nature delay the sale. Wraps for profit carry higher servicing risk and they demand greater investor-level sophistication and maturity along with significant financial resources.

Key components

- Title transfers to buyer.

- The Seller remains responsible for the original loan.

- End buyer pays seller or loan servicer, not original lender.

- The end buyer gains possession and resale rights.

- Two active obligations are layered through a single point of control.

Contractual and Ethical Boundaries

Wraps share the same inherent contractual tension associated with Subject-To transactions, the due-on-sale clause. The investor wrap for profit introduces an additional risk by adding a third party to the loan repayment stream. While I wholeheartedly encourage you to help sellers wrap their own mortgages, I suggest you apply a higher level of caution with wraps for profit.

My most significant concern, as it should by yours, is that the original seller's interest is not typically secured in these transactions. Without holding a promissory note secured by an all-inclusive deed of trust or wraparound mortgage, the seller has significantly less recourse in this type of transaction than in a simple Subject-To transaction. After speaking with several real estate attorneys, it might be theoretically possible to double-wrap a note, but it is fraught with complexity and potential legal landmines.

Risk Mitigation

If you choose to engage in this type of transaction as an agent, be certain that your brokerage supports it. Disclose all terms and roles transparently. Avoid acting as a principal and agent in the same transaction. Ensure that any investor or buyer is aware of due-on-sale risk and seller servicing obligations. Work only within your broker-approved frameworks. Use legal counsel for all documents beyond standard forms.

With respect to securing the original seller, wraps for profit are "backed by the full faith and credit of the investor," and nothing else. Therefore, you need to be vetting your investors carefully before engaging in these types of transactions. Verify that the investor you are working with has substantial assets including significant liquidity. Verify that they are experienced with this type of lending and that they are prepared to manage end buyer defaults. Speak to the investor's loan servicing company to verify both their experience and that they have a management plan in place.

Ensure that you act with full end-to-end transparency. Disclose all terms and roles. Inform all parties of the inherent risks. Confirm the investor's responsibility for defending a loan acceleration in the purchase contract. Do not engage with inexperienced investors.

Elements of the Contract

A proper wrap structure requires a new promissory note, a wraparound mortgage or all-inclusive deed of trust, allocation of defense responsibilities, appropriate disclosures, and essentially everything else you need for a Subject-To transaction with additional considerations such as:

- Title company that will provide title insurance for a wrap.

- Hazard and liability insurance with two additional insured parties.

Conclusion

Wraps for profit are not casual structures. They are engineered transactions that allow investors to generate yield. They demand full transparency, proper documentation, and legal awareness. These are not for speculative use or beginner improvisation. They engender additional risk when executed correctly, done improperly, they expose all parties to financial and legal harm.

Chapter 7:
Contract for Deed/Installment Sale

A contract for deed, also known as a land contract or installment sale contract, is a transitional ownership strategy. Note that I use these terms interchangeably in this text. This arrangement allows buyers to take possession and equitable title of a property while the seller retains legal title until full payment is made. This method is especially attractive in transactions where conventional financing is not available or appropriate. For brokers and agents navigating affordability gaps, investor-held properties, or hesitant sellers, the contract for deed can unlock otherwise inaccessible opportunities.

You cannot begin to have an intelligent conversation about installment sale contracts without having the context of the state in which the property is located. Of all available creative strategies, this is the one where rules vary the most from state to state. For sellers the allure of an installment sale contract is an assumption that the path to property forfeiture is easier, but this may be an illusion, or even an impediment, depending on the state.

Why use a Contract for Deed?

This arrangement creates an installment-based pathway to ownership, ideal for buyers needing seasoning time or sellers wanting to preserve title as security. When a buyer and seller sign an installment agreement, the buyer becomes the equitable owner of the property which could be land or land with a structure(s). Contract for deed is also frequently used for acquiring an easement.

The buyer can exercise agreed-upon rights of ownership, use, and enjoyment of the property during the term of the installment sale agreement. The seller enjoys the security of remaining on title. In some states, if the buyer fails to make payments in accordance with the terms of the installment agreement, the seller may be able to recover possession of the property quicker and at less expense than through the process of foreclosure, but in other states, such as California, repossessing property on an installment sale requires judicial foreclosure.

Unlike seller carrybacks with recorded trust deeds or mortgages, a contract for deed exists in a legal gray space in some states. Equity is conveyed contractually, not by deed. Therefore, due diligence and clear documentation are critical.

Installment Sale Contracts are particularly effective when:

- The seller prefers to hold title during the payment period.
- The buyer needs credit seasoning prior to obtaining conventional financing.
- You need to help someone with a VA loan sell with an existing purchase money loan as the Veteran's Administration does not classify installment sales as title alienation.

Advantages for Buyers and Sellers

For Buyers:

- No need to qualify for institutional financing.
- Immediate possession and control of the property.
- Opportunity to build equity while improving financial position.

For Sellers:

- Retains legal title until fully paid reducing risk.
- Potential tax deferral via installment sale reporting.
- Can structure terms to incentivize performance and protect asset.

Agents should position this strategy for buyers rebuilding credit, newly self-employed individuals, or investors acquiring properties in bulk without triggering lending thresholds.

Mechanics of Installment Sale Contracts

An installment sale agreement is an executory contract, a legally binding agreement where the parties have outstanding obligations yet to be fulfilled, meaning the contract is still in progress. The contract does not become fully executed until both parties fulfill all their obligations.

Key Components Include:

- Buyer takes possession and makes monthly payments directly to the seller.

- Seller retains legal title until all contract terms are satisfied.

- Title transfers only upon final payment, or at refinancing per agreement.

- Default remedies vary by state with some states allowing expedited forfeiture instead of formal foreclosure.

At first glance an installment sale contract appears to be less complex than a traditional sale, but the executory nature, duality of title, and enormous flexibility creates a proverbial iceberg of complexity below the surface. In creating an effective agreement, you must address questions such as:

- Party responsible for paying property taxes and insurance.

- Disposition of senior encumbrances.

- Additional lien restrictions.

- Payment structures and amortization rules.

These types of considerations are moot or well prescribed in other types of transactions, even with Subject-To. This is why it is desirable for both parties to have attorney representation.

You can set the amount and frequency of installments any way you choose in the installment agreement. The simplest approach is to structure an installment agreement exactly as you would a seller carryback by determining the sale price and down payment and then running an amortization to determine the monthly payment at a specified interest rate. Like a seller carryback you might specify a balloon payment required after some number of years. The only difference would be to cast it as an executory agreement rather than a sale where the title immediately transfers.

Issues to Address in an Installment Agreement

- Taxes. The installment seller remains the legal owner of the property on the public records including records of taxing authorities.

- Expenses: Allocate responsibilities to place deductible expenses (such as real estate taxes) with the taxpayer or structure the transaction to allow the non-taxpayer to seek a total or partial exemption from such taxes.

- Insurance: Because the title remains in the seller's name, the buyer should be added to the seller's policy as an additional insured. Consult an insurance professional before making any decisions.

- Maintenance: Because the buyer typically has full care, custody, and control of the property once the installment agreement is signed, the buyer typically assumes responsibility under the installment agreement to keep the property in good order and repair and in compliance with laws.

- Condemnation: If the property is condemned in whole or in part during the term of the installment agreement, both the installment seller and buyer will have claims for the taking of their respective interests in the property. The installment agreement should require the parties to cooperate with each other to obtain the full fair market value of the property taken and allocate the proceeds in accordance with a mutually agreeable formula.

Your buyer should be mindful that they are accepting the responsibilities of ownership without the security of title. The installment agreement should be very clear about how the parties will resolve any conflicts during the term of the Agreement. What constitutes an event of default? If the seller claims that the buyer is in default, what rights will be available to the Buyer? Will the buyer have an opportunity to cure an alleged default? Is the seller entitled to retain all of the amounts previously paid? What does governing state law have to say about these issues?

Risk Mitigation

When considering installment sale contracts, or other forms of executory contracts, your strongest risk management tool is to fully understand the impact of state laws. I repeat, of all creative financing strategies installment sale contracts and other executory contracts have the most variation in governing law from state to state.

Texas as Proxy for Legal Risk

The use of Texas in this section is intentional. Texas serves as a **proxy** for the kind of aggressive regulatory posture that other states may implement. While not every jurisdiction imposes the same constraints, treating Texas as a regulatory benchmark equips you to anticipate and navigate legal risk.

Laws are generally reactive, and it is evident that Texas statutes evolved from abuse of executory contracts by sellers. The following are highlights from Texas statute TITLE 2. CONVEYANCES CHAPTER 5. CONVEYANCES SUBCHAPTER A. GENERAL PROVISIONS:

Pre-Existing Purchase Money Liens: If the seller has a lien from a loan used solely to purchase the property, The seller must provide the buyer with a detailed written disclosure at least three days before executing the contract. This disclosure should include the lienholder's information, loan balance, payment terms, and a warning about potential foreclosure if payments are missed.

- The lien must pertain only to the property being sold and not exceed the buyer's total outstanding balance under the contract.

- The lienholder must consent to the executory contract and agree to verify loan status and accept direct payments from the buyer if the seller defaults.

- The contract must include covenants obligating the seller to make timely loan payments, provide monthly statements to the buyer, and notify the buyer of any default or foreclosure notices.

Buyer's Rights: Buyers have strong statutory protections under Texas law:

- Right to Cure Defaults: If a buyer defaults, they have a 30-day period to remedy the default before the seller can enforce remedies.

- Right to Convert Contract: At any time, a buyer can convert their interest into recorded legal title by tendering a promissory note equal to the remaining balance, prompting the seller to execute a deed and deed of trust.

- Right to Cancel: Buyers can cancel the contract for any reason within 14 days of signing.

- Right to Deduct: If the seller fails to comply with the contract, the buyer can deduct the amounts owed from payments due to the seller without judicial action.

Annual Accounting: Under Texas Property Code § 5.077, the seller must provide the buyer with an annual accounting statement for each year during the term of the contract. Failure to comply with this requirement may incur penalties. This statement must be delivered on or before January 31 of each year and must include:

- Amount paid under the contract.

- Amount still owed.

- Number of payments remaining.

- Amount paid in taxes and insurance.

- Delinquency information if any payments are overdue.

After reviewing these provisions, you might be wondering why a seller would choose this path. Because the buyer has a right to convert to a standard promissory note and deed of trust at will, why, indeed, would anyone choose an installment sale in Texas? As you might imagine, installment sale contracts are not a popular choice in Texas.

Elements of the Contract

You should treat an installment sale transaction with the same rigor that you apply to transaction where title transfers. Before entering into an installment agreement, your buyer should be satisfied that the property complies with applicable laws and there are no discoverable conditions that may result in unanticipated cost and expense.

Before entering into an installment agreement, the buyer should obtain a title commitment to insure their equitable ownership of the property under the installment sale agreement.

No mortgages or other liens should be permitted as exceptions to the title commitment unless there is an agreement between the buyer and the seller as to who is obligated to continue payments and remedies for failure to do so. The seller should be prohibited from further encumbering the property by mortgages or liens.

You should ensure that the installment agreement or a memorandum of the agreement is recorded promptly after signing. Typically, a memorandum, rather than the entire agreement, is recorded so as not to publicize the precise terms of payment or other private agreements of the parties, but some states require that you record the agreement. It should come as no surprise to you to learn that under Texas Property Code § 5.076, a seller is required to record an executory contract for conveyance of real property used or to be used as the purchaser's residence within 30 days of the date the contract is executed.

State-Level Considerations and Cautions

Contracts for deed are treated differently across state jurisdictions. The most challenging issue is that twenty-nine (29) states do not have specific statutory governance, at least none that I could find using AI to deep dive into this research. That leaves matters of property forfeiture governed under contract law and places all the burden on the integrity of the contract and the parties.

- Some states such as California treat them as equivalent to a mortgage and require formal foreclosure upon default. It is noteworthy that the CalVet home loan program uses this structure for its loans.

- Others allow forfeiture and cancellation of the contract and repossession often with minimal notice and process such as Arizona, although Arizona does require a judicial foreclosure after the buyer reaches a 25% payment threshold.

- Certain states such as Texas and Minnesota require special disclosures and statutory cancellation periods.

Do not use this structure casually. Always use attorney-prepared contracts. A thorough title search is essential. Ensure the contract includes:

- Clear payment terms and interest rate.

- Default and cure clauses.

- Provisions for property maintenance, insurance, and taxes.

- Protection for the buyer if the seller carries existing liens.

Appendix: The book download incudes a document detailing state-by-state installment sale protections and recording requirements.

A Transitional Strategy with Cautionary Edges

The contract for deed offers both a bridge and a buffer. For the right parties, in the right state, with the right contract, it is a powerful tool. Without legal alignment, it can quickly become a litigation trap. Always confirm state law. Always document clearly. Always disclose.

Chapter 8:
Lease Options, Lease Purchases & Master Leases

A lease is a contract between two parties, the **lessor** (landlord) and the **lessee** (tenant) that grants the lessee the right to use and occupy real property for a specified period of time in exchange for rent or other compensation. Leases allow investors to control properties without ownership, which is a powerful platform for building creative financing structures.

Why Lease Structures Matter

Lease structures such as lease options, lease purchases, and master leases offer scalable solutions for property acquisition. These instruments empower buyers to gain control and occupancy without immediate financing while providing sellers with income and strategic exit flexibility. Real estate professionals who understand these strategies elevate themselves from facilitators to opportunity architects capable of facilitating otherwise non-viable transactions.

Core Distinctions: Lease Option vs Lease Purchase

A lease option is a two-part arrangement in which the buyer (or tenant) leases the property with the right but not the obligation to purchase at a later date. If the buyer elects not to exercise the option, they can exit the arrangement without further obligation, though they typically forfeit any upfront option consideration. This structure offers flexibility to buyers and minimal enforcement risk for sellers.

Lease option transactions typically consist of two separate documents: a lease agreement and an option agreement. These should remain distinct to preserve the option's non-obligatory nature and to minimize the risk of regulatory misclassification. Key components of the lease agreement include the terms, monthly rent, maintenance responsibilities, and late fees. The option agreement should define the amount of non-refundable option consideration, the strike price (whether fixed or floating), the option period, and any assignability clauses. You must clearly state the means of serving notice and method of exercise.

In contrast, a lease purchase binds the buyer to purchase the property after a set period or upon satisfaction of predetermined conditions. The agreement outlines both the lease terms and the purchase mechanism. Because it imposes an obligation to purchase, this structure carries greater enforceability and potential legal exposure, especially if one party defaults.

Lease purchase agreements typically merge the lease and purchase elements into a single document or tightly linked contracts. This format often includes default remedies, closing timelines, and mechanisms for resolving disputes or enforcing purchase obligations. While lease purchases can offer clear paths to ownership, they can also attract greater legal scrutiny, and you should always consider having these reviewed by qualified counsel.

A master lease is a single lease agreement where the tenant, typically an investor or operator, leases an entire property or portfolio with rights to sublease all or parts of it. It is an excellent solution when the owner wants passive income, and the lessee desires to take control without an upfront purchase. Master leases are frequently used when properties are being repositioned for sale or redevelopment. When this is the objective, it is critical to confirm that zoning, subleasing rights, and local landlord-tenant laws permit this arrangement. Master leases should include detailed provisions about the purchase price, timelines, default consequences, and interim property management responsibilities.

Feature	Lease Option	Lease Purchase
Obligation to Buy	No	Yes
Strike Price	Usually Fixed	Fixed or Variable
Enforceability	Buyer-discretionary	Seller-enforceable
Buyer Risk	Low	High
Seller Remedies	Minimal	Full enforcement

Structural Components

Each of these lease variants have similar and distinctly different components and provisions.

Lease Purchase Agreement – Key Provisions

1. Parties Involved: Names and contact information of the lessor (seller) and lessee (buyer).

2. Legal Description of the Property Precise identification of the property being leased and sold.

3. Lease Terms: Duration, rent amount, payment due dates, and terms of occupancy.

4. Purchase Price: Fixed or formula-based price to be paid at the end of the lease term.

5. Purchase Commitment: Binding clause that obligates the tenant to purchase the property at lease end.

6. Down Payment or Earnest Money: Often non-refundable, applied toward the purchase.

7. Rent Credits (if any): Portion of rent applied toward the purchase price.

8. Default Provisions: Remedies and consequences if either party breaches the contract.

9. Closing Terms: How and when the closing will occur, who pays which costs.

10. Maintenance and Repairs: Defines which party is responsible during the lease term.

11. Possession and Risk of Loss: Clarifies when risk transfers and who holds insurance.

Lease Option Agreement – Key Provisions

1. Parties and Property Description: Same as above, with an added emphasis on separating lease and option terms.

2. Lease Terms: Duration, rent amount, and rules for use and maintenance.

3. Option to Purchase: Clear language stating the tenant has the right but not obligation to buy.

4. Option Period: Timeframe during which the option can be exercised.

5. Option Fee: Typically non-refundable, often credited toward purchase if exercised.

6. Purchase Price: Whether the price is pre-set or determined by appraisal must be clearly outlined.

7. Notice of Intent to Purchase: Procedure for the tenant to notify the landlord of intent to exercise the option.

8. Rent Credits (optional): Portion of rent applied to purchase price.

9. Conditions for Exercising Option: May include being current on rent, maintenance duties, or other performance benchmarks.

10. Default and Termination Clauses: What happens if either party defaults or if the option is not exercised.

Risk Mitigation

As a real estate professional and opportunity architect, I am always mindful of protecting both the buyer and the seller in a transaction. Avoiding blatantly unfair or imbalanced terms is as important as avoiding ambiguity. When contracts are fair and provide proper protection for everyone involved, disputes are less likely. That serves everyone's interest.

Tenant/Buyer Protections

Protection Type	Lease Purchase	Lease Option
Contingency Clauses	Financing, inspection, title issues	Financing, inspection, appraisal
Clear Purchase Terms	Fixed price or fair formula for final sale	Fixed price or option to match market
Equity Credit Language	Rent credits applied to purchase price	Optional rent credits specified clearly
Right to Cure Defaults	Grace periods for missed payments	Grace period for rent to preserve option
Maintenance Limits	Cap on tenant responsibility for repairs	Specify that landlord handles major repairs

Protection Type	Lease Purchase	Lease Option
Option Fee Clarity	Not applicable (unless a separate deposit)	Clarify amount, whether refundable/credited

Landlord/Seller Protections

Protection Type	Lease Purchase	Lease Option
Default Remedies	Clear path to reclaim possession or enforce sale	Specify forfeiture of option if breached
Option Expiry Terms	Not applicable	Deadline to exercise with formal notice
Occupancy Rules	Tenant responsibilities clearly defined	Same
Non-Assignment Clause	Prevent unauthorized transfer to third parties	Prevent unauthorized option transfer
Condition of Property	Inspection rights and maintenance expectations	Same
Insurance Requirement	Tenant carries renter's insurance	Same

Joint Protections

- Dispute Resolution Clause: Include mediation or arbitration to reduce litigation risks.

- State Law Compliance: Ensure agreement complies with local real estate and consumer protection laws.

- Recording (Strongly recommended): Record a memorandum of agreement to protect equitable interest (state-specific rules apply).

- Avoid combining lease and purchase into a single document.

- Use a third-party servicer or escrow for rent and option payments.

Positioning with Sellers and Landlords

From the seller's perspective, lease structures can offer attractive solutions. Sellers retain title while collecting rent and potential option consideration. They reduce or eliminate vacancy risk and can preserve depreciation deductions and defer capital gains tax until the property is sold. These structures are especially appealing to tired landlords or sellers struggling to find qualified buyers in a tight credit market.

When presenting these options, you should highlight income stability, minimized management burden, and tax benefits. Agreements should be structured so that the rent is slightly above market rates if credits are offered. Encourage sellers to use a third-party servicing company to collect rent and manage credits, adding professionalism and reducing dispute risk.

Buyer Considerations and Common Pitfalls

For buyers, lease structures provide access to homes without the burden of immediate financing. However, they must understand the limitations and risks. Buyers can lose their option consideration if they fail to exercise. Lease purchases may expose them to legal action if they default.

Another common issue is the lack of recorded documentation. If a lease option or purchase is not recorded, the buyer's equitable interest may be difficult to enforce. You must guide buyers to obtain legal advice, verify property condition, and ensure that all payments and credits are properly documented and serviced.

Ethical, Licensing Boundaries, and Compliance

Agents must operate within defined licensing parameters. You may act as agent, facilitator, or principal, provided that you disclose your role clearly. Do not draft complex agreements or collect fees outside the scope of licensure without explicit broker approval and full disclosure.

Be very cautious when advertising properties with creative terms. Federal laws such as the Truth in Lending Act (TILA) and Real Estate Settlement Procedures Act (RESPA) apply when advertising financing terms. Statements like "no credit check" or "seller financing available" should only be used if they are legally accurate and authorized by your broker.

Default and Exit Strategies

In lease options, if the buyer defaults by failing to pay rent or exercise the option, they typically forfeit their option fee and must vacate the property. In lease purchases, default may lead to a legal demand for specific performance or monetary damages.

To mitigate risk, contracts should include clear default clauses, cure periods, and remedies. If a lease-purchase deal begins to fail, it may be possible to convert it into a seller-financed transaction or land contract with mutual agreement. Your job is to anticipate such outcomes and have alternative paths pre-structured when feasible.

Master Leases and Master Lease Options

Master leases are typically used in commercial or multi-family residential contexts. They enable investors to control and operate a property without immediate ownership. In a master lease, the investor leases the entire property and gains the right to sublet individual units. The investor assumes responsibility for rent collection, maintenance, and often capital improvements.

Master lease options layer in the right to purchase the property after specific benchmarks are met, such as reaching a target occupancy or income level. These structures are particularly valuable for repositioning distressed or underperforming assets.

The benefits include avoiding lender financing, delaying capital gains events for sellers, and achieving high leverage with minimal upfront capital. However, they carry risks related to insurance, licensing, and legal enforceability. Agents involved in such transactions must ensure both parties understand subleasing terms and have legal support.

State-Level Restrictions and Executory Contract Considerations

Courts in numerous states may treat lease-purchase structures as executory contracts under state laws. An executory contract arises when a buyer gains equitable interest in the property without holding title. For instance, a court might interpret a large option fee as equity. This creates legal exposure and compliance requirements that vary by jurisdiction, and you should consider this a risk when dealing with residential property in every state.

Each state has its own unique laws. The callouts for the states that follow are by no means an exhaustive list of state-specific concerns.

Note: Given the variability in state laws, it's crucial to consult with a legal professional familiar with local real estate laws to navigate these agreements.

California

California has strict consumer protection laws and enforces rigorous disclosure requirements for real estate transactions, which can impact lease-to-own agreements. Courts may interpret long-term lease agreements with purchase options like installment sales, invoking foreclosure protections. Ensure that your lease agreements with purchase options are clearly documented, specifying terms, conditions, and disclosures.

Texas

Given what you learned about installment sales in Texas in the previous chapter, it should come as no surprise to you that similar equitable title issues cast a shadow on lease-purchase agreements. The Texas Property Code imposes specific requirements on executory contracts, affecting lease-to-own arrangements. To comply with executory contract laws, you must ensure that lease-purchase agreements adhere to Texas Property Code provisions, including mandatory disclosures and notices. Be prepared to follow formal foreclosure processes if the buyer defaults, as per Texas law.

Florida

In a dispute, Florida courts may classify lease-purchase agreements as either leases or sales contracts, affecting remedies when a tenant defaults. Agreements lacking clarity may be deemed unconscionable, leading to legal challenges. To avoid problems, your contract must define the nature of the agreement explicitly, outlining the rights and obligations of both parties. Ensure that the agreement is fair and transparent to withstand legal scrutiny as containing "unconscionable terms."

Illinois

If the agreement includes a binding obligation for the tenant to purchase the property, and both parties have significant unperformed obligations, it may be deemed an executory contract. If the purchase option is unilateral, meaning the tenant has the option but not the obligation to buy, the contract may not be considered executory until the option is exercised. Illinois imposes specific requirements for installment sales contracts, which can encompass lease-purchase agreements. For executory contracts, sellers must follow statutory procedures for default, including notices and potential foreclosure actions.

New York

New York courts may interpret lease-purchase agreements as equitable mortgages, invoking foreclosure protections for buyers. Consumer Protection Laws require disclosures and may affect the enforceability of certain lease-to-own contracts. Structure agreements to reflect their true nature Avoid unintended classifications that could trigger additional legal obligations.

Ohio

Ohio courts emphasize the "four corners" doctrine, meaning they interpret contracts strictly based on the written terms. Ambiguities or omissions can lead to unfavorable outcomes. Lease purchase agreements in Ohio may be recharacterized as installment contracts, which are subject to specific statutory requirements. Ohio has consumer protection laws that may apply to lease-to-own arrangements, especially if they are deemed to be in the nature of credit transactions.

You must ensure that your agreements contain precise language to reflect the true intent of the parties. Avoid ambiguities that could lead to recharacterization or misinterpretation. If the agreement resembles an installment contract, ensure compliance with relevant Ohio statutes, including disclosure requirements and remedies upon default.

Maryland

Maryland law requires specific disclosures in lease option agreements, including statements like "THIS IS NOT A CONTRACT TO BUY" and references to applicable statutes. Failure to include these can render the agreement voidable. Options to purchase that extend beyond certain timeframes may violate Maryland's *Rule Against Perpetuities*, potentially rendering them void. Agreements lacking clarity or fairness may be deemed unconscionable, leading to legal challenges.

Ensure all lease option agreements contain the mandated statements as per Maryland. Code, Real Property § 8-202. Structure purchase options to be exercisable within timeframes that comply with the *Rule Against Perpetuities* to avoid invalidation. Your contract must have clear and fair terms to withstand scrutiny and avoid being deemed unconscionable.

Impacts of Bankruptcy

Timing Matters when a tenant declares bankruptcy. Whether the tenant/debtor has exercised an option or defaulted pre-bankruptcy affects classification. Clearly structured agreements help courts and parties determine appropriate bankruptcy treatment. Because state law governs the nature of individual's interest in real estate interpretations can vary.

Tenant Bankruptcy

The tenant's obligations (to lease, buy, or exercise an option) become part of the bankruptcy estate.

The tenant/debtor has the power, subject to court approval, to:

- Assume or reject executory contracts such as lease options or lease purchase agreements.
- Cure defaults under an installment sale if it's treated as a secured transaction.
- Or retain property under Chapter 13 if they continue payments.

Seller/Landlord Bankruptcy

The buyer's or tenant's rights are generally protected under bankruptcy law. If the tenant is in possession, the seller's bankruptcy cannot cancel the agreement unilaterally. Under 11 U.S.C. § 365(i), if a seller (landlord) rejects a lease-purchase or installment sale agreement, and the buyer is in possession, the buyer can:

- Retain possession and make payments.

- Offset damages if the seller fails to perform.

- If the option to purchase has been exercised, the buyer may be able to enforce it even if the seller enters bankruptcy.

Conclusion

Because executory contracts draw additional scrutiny in numerous states where additional consumer protection laws come into play, you might want to consider working mainly with lease-options, rather than lease-purchase agreements. Make certain that you work with an attorney to determine what works best in the state where you practice.

Chapter 9:
Lease Purchase Option Method

(Formerly "Novation")

For years, a specific creative finance strategy has been misbranded in investor circles as a "novation." In reality, these transactions do not meet the legal or contractual definition of a novation. What investors want is something else entirely; a structured framework that enables them to control, improve, and profit from a property without ever owning it. I call this model the **Lease Purchase Option (LPO) Method** and it is time to embrace it with the formality and clarity it deserves.

Defining the Lease Purchase Option method (LPO)

In this chapter I define the LPO method, contrast it with the flawed so-called "novation" approach, and provide you with the tools to understand, vet, and participate in this advanced investment strategy ethically and legally.

A Lease Purchase Option Agreement is a three-document transaction model designed to give investors control over a property for the purpose of executing renovations and exiting through resale. The structure allows for lawful possession, operational improvement, and coordinated disposition without requiring title transfer or bank financing at the outset.

I developed this solution inspired by the forms provided by the California Association of Realtors. I must tip my hat to the agents who volunteer to serve on Forms Advisory Committee and the attorneys from the C.A.R. Legal team for the incredibly comprehensive forms library they provide. I purposely connected with agents around the country who have kindly indulged my forms voyeurism tour, and I can say with certainty that California agents have a significant advantage. If you rely on forms in other states, you will likely need to make an investment in legal services to supplement what you have at hand. The elegant three-document solution that supports the LPO method deploys three legal documents:

1. **Lease Agreement** – grants the investor legal possession and access to the property and conveys the right to renovate the property.

2. **Purchase Agreement** – contains final price and terms, typically held in escrow and triggered by exercise of the option.

3. **Option Agreement** – provides the investor exclusive right, but not obligation, to purchase the property. It echoes the renovation rights and contains language to modify the lease and purchase agreements upon exercise.

Lease Agreement: I typically calculate the monthly rent in the lease agreement by covering all costs for the seller including mortgage payment(s), utilities, HOA fees, leased items such as solar or water systems, and utilities. One of your first steps is to discover and quantify all costs. Depending on the seller's situation, you may want to include additional cash flow for the seller, keeping in mind that you can credit a portion of the rent to the purchase price. The lease agreement should contain language that grants the lessee rights to renovate the property. At the very least it should have language similar to the following:

- Lessor acknowledges that it is Lessee's expressed intent to improve the property and resell it for a profit.

- Lessor grants permission to Lessee to perform repairs to the property both minor and major at Lessee's sole discretion.

Purchase Agreement: You should create a standard purchase agreement using the same form and format that you typically use. There is nothing special about this document, it should reflect the price the investor pays to the seller for the property and include normal contingencies if required.

Option Agreement: I get resistance from real estate professionals and investors alike when I prescribe a separate document for the option. "It's a lease purchase, that's one document," they insist. "Well, yes, you can certainly have that all in one document," I respond, "but the magic formula is to separate them." The magic of the separate option agreement is that it serves as interstitial tissue connecting the lease agreement and the purchase agreement. It legally incorporates the other two agreements by reference.

The option agreement describes what happens to the lease agreement and the purchase agreement when the investor exercises the option. For instance, it contains a provision that all of the time limits contained in the purchase agreement, which begin on the date of acceptance, will instead begin to run from the date that the option is exercised. It explains how the lease will be retired upon recordation of the sale of the property.

When I write the option agreement, I echo the provisions that I include in the lease agreement as stated previously. I add additional language as follows:

- Optionor grants Optionee permission to market the property at Optionee's sole discretion including listing the property on the MLS.

- Optionor agrees to sign a Listing Agreement and other Documents and Agreements that may be necessary to support Optionee's marketing efforts.

You can opt to have the seller sign the listing agreement at the time you execute the three core documents if you know the listing price, or you can wait until the property is ready to market. Although it may make some investors nervous to wait to have this document signed, any agent should know why doing this in advance is challenging considering MLS rules and considering that a listing agreement becomes a living contract once signed and must be managed as such going forward including executing amendments when timelines or prices change.

Why the LPO Method is not a Novation

A true novation involves a full substitution of contractual parties with the release of prior obligations. Most investors using the term "novation" are instead stepping into the deal as an intermediary and marketing the property before they hold title. This is not a novation, which creates serious legal vulnerabilities.

In the misbranded novation model, the investor typically uses power of attorney (POA) signed by the seller to list and market the property. This is a red flag. A POA holder has a fiduciary duty to act in the best interest of the seller (principal). As the buyer, that same person also has a personal interest in securing favorable terms for themselves. This duality inherently conflicts with their duty to the seller as a fiduciary.

Using a POA to market and sell a property you do not own creates a self-dealing risk, especially if the investor is licensed or using an affiliated agent. Courts often presume that a POA holder has undue influence when engaging in such transactions. In many states, transactions where an agent under POA benefits personally can be voided or reversed, especially if challenged by the seller or their heirs. In contrast, the LPO method gives the investor written, layered, and enforceable rights without the need for a POA or what might be considered as deceptive positioning.

Using the LPO method, there are no party substitutions or assignments. The investor is not released from any duties under the contract. Instead, the investor maintains legal control through leasehold, a secured right to purchase through an option and a signed purchase agreement, and fully disclosed resale intent anchored by three connected agreements containing specific contractual provisions.

Three Parties, Two Transactions, One Closing

The ultimate advantage of only **one closing** is that it reduces transactional money costs, direct transactional costs, and streamlines the process by allowing renovations to begin concurrently with opening escrow. The transactional flow is as follows:

1. Investor (Party B) signs Lease + Option + Purchase Agreement with Original Seller (Party A). The agent opens an escrow for the A to B transaction and the investor deposits EMD. This will be a longer that usual escrow because it encompasses both the renovation period and the eventual marketing and sales period.

2. The investor (Party B) takes possession and renovates under rights established in the leasehold and option agreement. As the renovation comes to a close, you have the Seller (Party A) sign a listing agreement and the agent performs all the necessary and typical preparations for marketing the home including photography, video, and staging.

3. The agent markets the improved property and presents offers until one is ultimately selected and a purchase agreement is signed between the investor (Party B) and the end buyer (Party C). The agent opens an escrow for the B to C transaction with the same escrow company. The normal real estate purchase process ensues until the end buyer releases all contingencies, escrow is perfected and all parties, A, B, C, and their respective agents are ready to close.

4. At the closing, the investor exercises the option, the lease is terminated, and both purchase agreements are closed using the funding from the end buyer in a simultaneous or sequential (waterfall) close.

5. The original seller receives the purchase price they accepted in the initial agreement plus any additional funds that may have been provided in the lease agreement, and the investor captures the spread or equity gain from the renovation value-add. The flow is illustrated in Figure 9-1.

LPO Method

LEASE AGREEMENT		OPTION AGREEMENT		PURCHASE AGREEMENT
• Investor leases property	→	• Exclusive right to purchase property	→	• Final price and terms set
• Right to renovate granted		• Investor may market property		• Held in escrow

• Renovations are completed
• Option is exercised

LPO METHOD

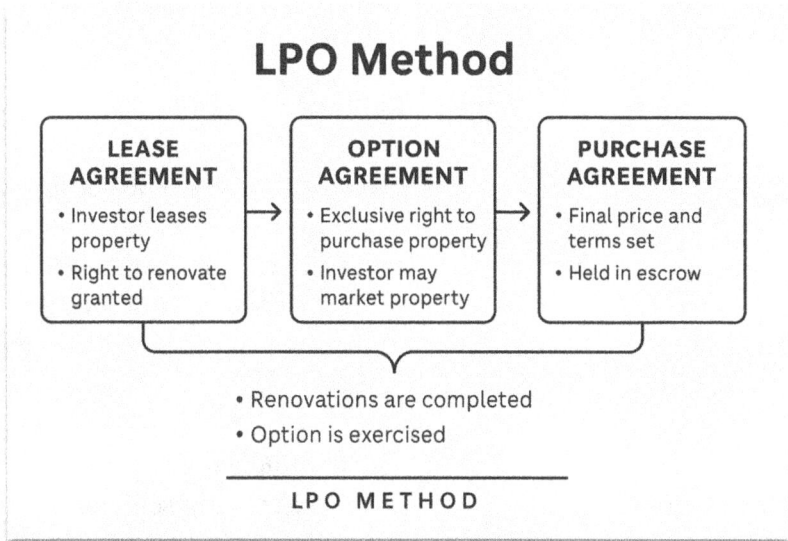

Figure 9-1: LPO Method flow.

Perhaps the most strategically unique aspect of the LPO Method is that it enables participation by three distinct brokerages across a single transaction lifecycle: (1) the **Seller's Agent**, (2) the **Investor's Agent**, and (3) the **End Buyer's Agent**. The investor's agent occupies a dual role representing the investor as a buyer in the initial acquisition and as a seller in the subsequent resale. While this configuration introduces opportunities for coordinated execution and broader market exposure, it also presents a theoretical scenario in which a single licensee could represent all three parties. The very notion of "triple-ending" a deal should raise immediate ethical red flags. Such an arrangement, although not impossible, is fraught with conflicts of interest. You should approach this with extreme caution, full disclosure, and only after documented clearance with the compliance department at your brokerage.

CART Evaluation: LPO Method

Lever	Score	Rationale
Control	5	Investor takes legal possession, recorded option rights, renovation and resale authority, and contractual exclusivity. Despite lacking title, the structure achieves full operational and economic control.
Access to Capital	5	No new financing required. Investor leverages existing seller obligations and uses contract rights in place of traditional funding.
Risk Allocation	4	Investor bears renovation and resale execution risk; seller retains title risk. Clear contractual boundaries and escrowed documents mitigate exposure for both the investor and the seller.
Terms	4	Highly customizable structure using three separate agreements (lease, option, and purchase). Investor can set rent, purchase price, option timeline, and exit terms flexibly.

Total Score: 18 / 20 - Strategically powerful control structure enabling resale and renovation without ownership. Execution risk remains high without legal title, requiring experienced legal drafting and strict seller alignment.

Risk Mitigation

The obvious inherent risk in this strategy is that the investor is renovating a property they do not own. Providing that all parties remain committed to the arrangement, and the investor performs, the likelihood of realizing this risk is limited, but the risk is real. A misbehaving seller can create obstacles to closing. Best practices include the following:

- Record a memorandum of the option agreement to protect the investor's equitable interest.

- The seller must vacate the property. If your seller needs additional funds to support a move or temporary housing, you need to accommodate them or do not do the project. If the property has an ADU that is not impacted by the renovations, it is possible to allow that tenant to remain on the property.

- Using the LPO method for residential real estate is most appropriate for projects up to 180 days. It is worth noting that Texas has a carveout in its executory contract regulations for agreements where the intent is to deliver a deed within 180 days. You should understand your state-specific requirements for equitable interest, escrow, and marketing rights.

- If you are acting as an agent for the investor in a transaction like this, make sure you qualify your investor client. Verify their ability to complete both the renovation and the transaction.

- Educate all parties on legal distinctions between control and ownership.

- Purchase necessary builder's risk insurance.

What you must not do is act as a silent participant in a transaction that misuses paperwork, especially POAs, to mask the true structure of the deal. The LPO method brings sunlight and defensibility to what is otherwise a hazy and risky practice.

Conclusion: Why the LPO Method is the Future

The LPO method is more than just a renamed structure, it is a response to the legal, ethical, and operational flaws embedded in today's so-called novation templates. By anchoring the agreement in a lease, an option, and a purchase contract, and by abandoning risky POAs and party substitution gimmicks, the LPO offers a legally clean, repeatable model.

Chapter 10:
Understanding Capital

Real estate professionals working with real estate investors must understand that the most decisive factor in whether a deal closes is not price, it is capital. Capital moves deals. Capital decides timing. And capital, when sourced creatively, becomes the bridge between buyer intent and seller urgency. In this environment, where traditional lending continues to constrict under the weight of regulatory scrutiny, and risk-based pricing, the agent who can connect to non-bank capital becomes indispensable.

Private money and hard money are no longer fringe tools used only by flippers. They are now central to deal flow across a wide range of scenarios: buyers with non-conforming income, investors seeking fast close timelines, sellers looking to unlock liquidity before stabilization, and even homeowners navigating transitional life events. The speed and flexibility of this capital cannot be matched by conventional mortgage products. In some cases, deals exist solely because private capital agrees to fund them.

The investor market requires a velocity and flexibility of funding that traditional institutional capital cannot reliably meet. Investors are unwilling to wait 30 or 45 days to learn that a loan will not fund. They need certainty. Hard money, particularly when sourced from experienced institutional providers or pre-committed private investors, delivers that certainty. It allows an agent or investor to move with confidence, not speculation.

It is not sufficient for you to know that private money exists. You must understand the ethical, legal, and financial nuances that govern its use. Not all money is equal. The difference between a compliant capital relationship and an illegal securities offering may be a single misplaced good intention. The distinction between bridging a deal and brokering a loan without a license may be one sentence in an email or text. You must operate inside the boundaries while thinking outside the box.

In this chapter, I dissect the various sources of private and hard money, clarify the distinction between institutional and private hard money, and equip you to ethically structure, position, and navigate these relationships. I show you how to package deals for capital partners, how to avoid common compliance traps, and how to frame your value as a conduit of positive outcomes.

Capital is no longer just a closing table issue. It is now a listing strategy, a buyer conversion tool, and an agent differentiator. Your mastery of creative capital sources defines whether you are merely part of the transaction or the reason it happened.

Understanding the Difference Between Private and Hard Money

Before you can effectively operate in the private capital space, you must develop fluency in its language. Private money and hard money are often used interchangeably in conversation, obscuring their critical differences. While both fall outside of conventional institutional financing, their mechanics, motivations, and legal implications diverge in ways that matter.

Private Money

Private money refers to funds loaned by individuals or small entities most often within the borrower's personal or professional network. These lenders are not in the business of lending per se. They are capital holders, family members, friends, retired professionals, or high-net-worth acquaintances interested in returns secured by real estate. The underwriting in these cases is relational. Decisions are made based on trust, clarity of presentation, and the credibility of the borrower or operator. Terms may be generous or strict, but they are not dictated by institutional overlays. Instead, they emerge from negotiation.

Hard Money

Hard money is typically offered by firms whose primary business is lending against real estate. These are asset-based lenders. They evaluate properties and projects as much as they do people. Creditworthiness is definitely considered, but the primary criteria is the protective equity in the deal. Hard money lenders charge higher interest rates, impose points, and often include origination or servicing fees. The trade-off is speed, flexibility, and a willingness to fund deals that conventional lenders will not touch.

There is a gray zone where private money and hard money overlap. Some lenders market themselves as private but operate as hard money shops with licensed teams, defined underwriting protocols, and regulatory oversight. Others function as unregulated capital aggregators raising funds through crowdfunding platforms, pooled investor groups, or even note syndications, and then lending them through hard money-style instruments. These hybrid models complicate the landscape and increase compliance risk.

As a licensed real estate professional, the distinction is not merely semantic, it determines your level of risk, the disclosure obligations you must meet, and the licensing boundaries you cannot cross. You may introduce a buyer to a private lender you know personally, but if you are compensated for doing so, you likely crossed into unlicensed mortgage brokering. You may introduce a hard money lender to a client, but if you negotiate terms or influence underwriting, you risk acting beyond the scope of your license. Unless you have a Mortgage Loan Originator (MLO) endorsement on your license, you should think of your role as a "connector."

Earlier this year I stepped into a deal where another agent had alienated a client who I worked with on the sale of her primary residence. While evaluating the deal I realized that she had not yet secured the funding needed to close, so I introduced her to a hard money lender that I worked with on previous projects, Kiavi (formerly Lending Home). When the underwriting looked a little rocky a week later, I was able to provide the comps and the reasoning to substantiate the project after repair value

(ARV). I was not compensated for the funding acrobatics, but I did save and close a two-million-dollar deal.

Within the hard money space, you will encounter two distinct species of capital operating under the same banner: **institutional hard money** and **private hard money**. To the untrained eye, both offer fast, flexible financing outside traditional lending models. But for an agent navigating creative finance, the difference is foundational. Each source carries unique implications for deal flow and borrower experience.

Institutional hard money refers to capital deployed through licensed entities, which are typically corporations or funds registered in multiple states. The capital partner I mentioned previously, Kiavi, is such a lender. These firms maintain formal underwriting departments, standardized processes, and regulatory oversight. They often have a range of products for investors and developers and their timelines are rapid, particularly for repeat customers that establish a strong track record. These lenders thrive on repeat business with investors and agents who operate at volume. Because of this, institutional hard money tends to be more reliable.

Borrowers engaging institutional lenders encounter defined loan-to-value thresholds, required appraisals, title insurance mandates, and disclosures designed to mirror portions of the consumer lending process, even when not strictly required by law. These lenders prioritize execution. The borrower is expected to provide a completed package, which is often facilitated by a sophisticated online intake process. There is limited room for creative structuring or subjective decision-making. Institutional hard money is capitalized efficiency.

Private hard money originates from individuals or small capital pools that operate outside of a licensed lending framework. These lenders may be retired investors, family offices, or informal partnerships with real estate experience and a desire for yield. Their underwriting is personal, often guided by relationships, perceived borrower competence, and collateral quality. A private lender may fund a deal based on a conversation and a spreadsheet. They may waive inspections, accept unorthodox terms, or participate in a joint venture model rather than a note-and-deed structure.

This flexibility comes with trade-offs. Private hard money is inconsistent by nature. One lender's risk tolerance may differ dramatically from another's. Documentation quality varies. Enforcement mechanisms may be unclear. And in the absence of a formal servicing process, the burden of communication and compliance may fall squarely on the borrower's shoulders.

For agents, the distinction shapes how you introduce, advise, and protect your clients. If you refer a buyer to an institutional hard money lender, you can rely on established processes and legal guardrails. You must still provide disclosures and avoid brokering loans without proper licensure, but the systemic risk is lower. When you engage a private hard money lender, particularly someone who is unfamiliar with regulatory boundaries, you must proceed with heightened diligence. Ensure that all roles are disclosed, documents are professionally prepared, and that both parties understand the legal implications of the structure.

Sourcing Private Capital Ethically and Legally

It is not difficult to find money. It is difficult to source capital that is both legally compliant and ethically sound. In the world of creative real estate, private capital offers enormous potential and enormous exposure. You must understand the regulatory landscape around capital sourcing, or you risk violating both licensing law and federal securities statutes. Note that your brokerage may have specific restrictions on referring lenders.

Start with this foundational truth: private capital is not unregulated. While it may operate outside traditional banking frameworks, it remains subject to the Securities Act of 1933, which governs the offer and sale of investment instruments in the United States. When a real estate transaction involves soliciting money in exchange for a promised return, particularly when the money investor plays no active role in managing the investment, you may be offering a security. And offering a security without registration or exemption is a federal offense.

Syndications, SEC Rules, and Your Boundaries

A syndication is a formalized investment structure where multiple investors pool capital to acquire and operate real estate assets. These structures often operate through limited liability companies or limited partnerships, where one party (or group), the General Partner (GP) manages the asset, and the rest of the investors are Limited Partners (LPs) are passive. The distinction is legal not academic. The moment you solicit, promote, or accept capital from others for shared profits, you may be operating within the domain of securities law.

There are to primary legal exemptions used in real estate found in Regulation D under SEC Rule 506(b) and Rule 506(c). These allow for the private offering of securities without registration, provided the capital is raised under specific limitations. For example, under Rule 506(b), you may raise money from an unlimited number of accredited investors and up to 35 non-accredited, but you may not publicly advertise the offering. The exemption requires a pre-existing relationship and substantive vetting. It is not enough to meet someone at a conference or through a social media post. The relationship must predate the solicitation.

Rule 506(b): The Quiet Offering

Under 506(b), syndicators may raise an unlimited amount of capital from accredited investors and up to 35 non-accredited sophisticated investors, but they may not advertise or solicit publicly. No social media posts. No email blasts. No casual forwarding of flyers to your client list.

All investors must have a pre-existing, substantive relationship with the syndicator. Furthermore, syndicators are not required to verify an investor's accreditation status; they may rely on self-certification under a reasonable belief standard.

If you email or share a deal that turns out to be a 506(b) offering and someone invests because of your message, you may have just facilitated an unregistered securities offering whether you were compensated or not.

Rule 506(c): The Public Raise

In contrast, 506(c) allows general solicitation, meaning that operators can publicly advertise. However, they may only accept accredited investors, and accreditation must be verified through tax returns, W-2s, or third-party certifications (CPA, attorney, broker-dealer). There is no allowance for non-accredited investor participation under this rule.

This model is safer for agents to share, but only if you are not compensated and not involved in investor verification, marketing design, or capital negotiations. Your role must remain that of a connector, not a syndication participant.

I recently had the pleasure of speaking with Brenda Jones on my weekly zoom/podcast call. Brenda and her partners had just completed raising money with their first fund to purchase an RV park in Texas and was only several days away from closing when we spoke. Her insights were fresh and her enthusiasm vivid in relating her experience with the process. "It's developing relationships. It's not asking for money. You're showing people an opportunity. You're giving them an opportunity to make more money than the stock market," she said as she began describing her experience with creating a fund under 506(c), which they chose because it was less restrictive of public promotion and allows finding investors outside of existing relationships. Advertising includes talking about your fund on social media.

"It really is all about building relationships. The majority of the people we raised money from are people we already knew and with whom we have established trust relationships. Going forward, I need to do more re-lationship building if I want to raise money from people I do not already know."

"Once we got something under contract, we started calling everyone and texting them to start having more specific conversations. The first step was inviting them all to our investors zoom, where we actually went over our pitch deck, broke everything down and presented the deal in detail. And then after that was just, again, a lot of chasing, even though there were people that we knew, we still had to chase them to sign the paperwork."

Nonetheless, Brenda and her partners were successful in raising $1.7 million dollars for their first venture. When I asked her how much up-front investment there was to launch the fund, she said that $10,000 to $20,000 is required as well as engaging with a company to verify investors.

General Partnerships and the Dangerous Grey Zone

In smaller or emerging syndications, you may encounter an offer like, "Bring in a few investors and we'll give you a slice of the GP." This is called a Co-GP structure, and it is a legal minefield if not properly documented. For a Co-GP to be legitimate, you must contribute **active value** such as op-erational oversight, underwriting, construction supervision, or loan guar-antees. Merely introducing capital is not sufficient.

If your sole contribution is access to investors, then you are likely engaging in unlicensed capital raising, which violates both federal securities law and agent licensing statutes in most states.

Your role, as an agent, must remain advisory when introducing capital to a transaction. You may point a client toward a private lender you know. You may facilitate an introduction. But you may not promise returns, struc-ture the loan, or receive a fee based on loan placement unless you are li-censed as a mortgage broker or have obtained explicit broker and attorney approval. Even in jurisdictions where agents are permitted to collect consulting fees, the purpose, disclosure, and recipient of that fee must be crystal clear.

Unless you are starting a fund compliant with SEC rules, your best posture is this; You are not raising capital, rather you are presenting deals. Let the capital find you. Let relationships precede opportunity. Let your value be the clarity with which you present structure, not the capital itself. When you behave like a deal architect rather than a capital middleman, you maintain the ethical high ground and reduce compliance friction.

Above all, avoid general solicitation. Do not post investment opportunities with projected returns on social media unless you are working under a registered offering or partnering with a licensed entity that handles all securities compliance. Do not promise investors passive income unless the deal has been vetted by a securities attorney. And do not take investor money into your own account under any circumstances. Even if the intent is innocent, the implications are not.

What Regulation D Actually Enables

Regulation D is often perceived as legal quicksand, but that perception masks a powerful truth. If structured properly, Reg D offerings, especially 506(b) and 506(c), allow investors to legally raise significant capital from private individuals without becoming securities brokers or licensed investment advisors.

506(b) enables relationship-driven syndications. You cannot advertise, but you can raise from up to 35 non-accredited investors, plus unlimited accredited investors, provided you can prove a pre-existing substantive relationship.

506(c) removes the relationship requirement but restricts you to accredited investors only and requires verification.

These exemptions do not require pre-approval from the SEC but do require rigorous documentation and compliance protocols. Use competent legal counsel to build your framework. Once established, you can repeat and scale it.

Bottom Line: Regulation D is not just for hedge funds. It is a capital unlock for investors who are ready to level up and follow the rules.

Crowd Funding

Regulation Crowdfunding (Reg CF) is a U.S. Securities and Exchange Commission (SEC) rule that allows startups and small businesses to raise capital from a large number of investors through online platforms. It was created under the Jumpstart Our Business Startups (JOBS) Act of 2012.

Reg CF allows private companies to raise up to $5 million annually by offering securities (e.g., equity, debt) to both accredited and non-accredited investors via a registered funding portal or broker-dealer.

Key Features

- Annual Raise Limit: Up to $5 million per 12-month period.

- Investor Limits are based on income or net worth.

- If either annual income or net worth is less than $124,000, the investment limit is 5% of the lesser of income or net worth.

- If both are $124,000 or more, the limit is 10% of the lesser of income or net worth.

- Cap: No individual can invest more than $124,000 in Reg CF offerings per year.

Issuers must use a registered funding portal such as Wefunder, StartEngine, Republic, or a broker dealer. Disclosure Requirements include basic information on the company's business, financials, use of funds, ownership, and risks. The financial statements may need to be reviewed or audited depending on the amount raised. Securities purchased in a Reg CF offering generally cannot be sold for one year, with some exceptions. Advertising these is limited. Issuers can generally share only a "tombstone" ad with basic facts and a link to the portal.

Use Cases

Crowd funding is ideal for startups, small businesses, and social enterprises seeking to raise early capital while building a base of engaged supporters and investors. Several notable success stories include Mercury Banking for Startups. Mercury, a financial services provider tailored for startups, leveraged Reg CF to engage a broad investor base. The successful campaign on Wefunder demonstrated the potential of equity crowdfunding for fintech companies. Mercury raised $4.9 million from 2,453 investors at a valuation of $1.62 billion. LiquidPiston, specializing in innovative engine designs, nearly reached the Reg CF maximum funding limit, raising $4.97 million on Deal Maker, reflecting strong investor interest in advanced engineering solutions.

Watch for Innovators

A new company called Fractional is making waves in the fundraising industry. It stands out as an innovator in the real estate investment landscape by combining legal structuring, community engagement, and technological automation. Its model lowers barriers to entry, promotes collaborative ownership, and streamlines the investment process, making it a noteworthy option for individuals seeking to enter the real estate market through fractional ownership.

Innovative Use of LLC Structures

Fractional facilitates the creation of a separate Limited Liability Company (LLC) for each property investment. This structure offers several benefits:

- Liability Protection: Each property is isolated within its own LLC, safeguarding investors from liabilities associated with other properties or the platform itself.

- Simplified Management: The LLC framework allows for organized management of finances, operations, and legal matters specific to each property.

- Clear Ownership Stakes: Investors hold membership interests in the LLC, providing a transparent and legally recognized ownership structure.

This approach ensures that each investment is compartmentalized, reducing risk and enhancing clarity for co-owners.

Community-Centric Investment Model

Fractional emphasizes building communities around each investment opportunity featuring collaborative decision making. Co-owners engage in collective decisions regarding property management, renovations, and rental strategies. It attracts multiple skillsets where investors contribute various expertise to each project through shared goals and aligned interests. Co-owners work together to achieve common financial and operational objectives, fostering a sense of partnership and shared responsibility among investors.

Streamlined Investment Process

Fractional simplifies the real estate investment process through its platform. Users initiate investment opportunities and raise funds from their networks with investments starting as low as $5,000.00. The platform assists with legal compliance, LLC formation, and necessary documentation. The platform automations include automated distributions, tax document generation (e.g., K-1s), and voting mechanisms for property decisions. These tools reduce administrative burdens and make real estate investment more accessible.

How Tiny Investors Close Big Deals

Traditional financing requires one big check. Companies like Fractional turn that model inside out. With tools like partial note sales, micro-syndications, and real estate crowdfunding platforms, dealmakers can now aggregate many small investors to fund a transaction without institutional support.

Imagine a scenario where a $400,000 investment property is funded by eight investors contributing $50,000 each. Each investor holds a fractional promissory note or equity share. A servicing agent or platform distributes payments or profits proportionally.

These are no longer theoretical models, they are operational frameworks supported by escrow technology, online investor portals, and SEC-compliant templates. You do not need exotic technologies like blockchain to fractionalize. You simply need structure.

It Matters **because** this level of access to capital expands your reach. You no longer need a whale investor. You need a school of minnows and a way to organize them.

Your Boundaries in Syndication Contexts

Action	Permissible?	Notes
Introducing a deal sponsor to a client.	Yes	With clear disclosure, no compensation tied to capital raised.
Advise a client to invest in a syndication.	Risky	Must be framed as general info. Avoid language implying suitability.

Action	Permissible?	Notes
Receive equity in exchange for bringing investors.	No	Unless fully registered and documented as a GP with operational duties.
Help design offering materials or pitch decks.	No	Considered active participation in a securities offering.
Participating as a passive LP.	Yes	As a personal investor, not in your licensed capacity.

Conclusion: The Capital Connector Mindset

Creative financing is both a skillset and a mindset. It is not about exotic deal structures or clever term sheets. It is about knowing how capital thinks. It is about knowing what makes money move and what makes it stay away. More than any other professional in the real estate transaction, an agent has the unique opportunity to become a trusted capital connector.

The purpose of this chapter is to help you recognize power. In real estate, power belongs to those who can mobilize capital ethically, structure deals responsibly, and guide clients through creative options without crossing into unauthorized practice. Power belongs to those who protect investor interests while still advocating for buyers and sellers. It belongs to those who know how to create a structure that works and stays compliant.

You must reimagine your identity. You are no longer simply an agent who transacts, you are a manager of leverage. You are the person who keeps deals alive when others give up. You are the person who does not flinch when financing falls through because you have access to alternatives.

You now know how private money differs from hard money. You understand institutional versus private hard capital. You learned about crowdfunding and syndication, and you know how to keep your eye out for innovative startups like Fractional that can assist your investor clients connect to the capital they require. You can identify red flags, avoid regulatory pitfalls, and build relationships that endure. That makes you indispensable.

The trust you build with private capital partners is not founded on yield; it is based on stewardship. The investors who stay with you over time will be the ones who see that you protect their interests with as much vigilance as your own.

Real estate is changing. Capital is becoming decentralized. Traditional financing will never fully return to its former simplicity. But that is not a limitation. It is an opportunity for those who know how to move in the shadows between bank and borrower, between asset and investor, between possibility and execution.

CART Evaluation: By Capital Source

In this case, scoring is for a single lever for each capital strategy.

Capital Source	Access Score	Commentary
Conventional Bank Financing	1	Rigid underwriting, high documentation, low adaptability
Seller Carryback	3	Flexible, but limited by seller's risk tolerance and equity position.

Capital Source	Access Score	Commentary
Private Money (Personal)	4	Trust-based, fast, adaptable, but inconsistent in structure and enforceability.
Hard Money (Institutional)	3	Reliable timelines and processes, but costlier and bound by compliance.
Hard Money (Private)	4	More flexible than institutional, but varies widely in process and professionalism.
Reg D 506(b)	4	High access with relationship constraints; ideal for repeat capital partners.
Reg D 506(c)	5	Maximum capital reach via public advertising; highly structured.
Syndication	5	Syndications pool private investor capital without relying on institutional lending.
Fractional Capital or Crowdfund	5	Most scalable, adaptable, and accessible to retail investors when legally structured.

Chapter 11:
Creating Partnerships and Equity Splits

Creative finance does not end with the structure of the deal. It extends into the structure of partnerships. Many of the agents I know, and meet through transactional encounters, are increasingly curious about or eager to become investors themselves. This often involves participation in partnerships with investors, operators, and capital contributors. Whether through sweat equity, direct investment, or resource alignment, these partnerships create opportunity and risk. To structure these relationships properly, you must understand the legal, ethical, and practical implications of shared ownership, shared returns, and shared control.

Your capital may not be cash. It might be time, expertise, licensing, deal flow, or construction management, also known as "sweat equity." When you contribute value without formalizing terms, you place yourself at significant legal and financial risk. In this chapter I provide you with considerations for structuring partnerships and equity participation models in a way that protects your license and your upside.

Joint Venture Agreements (JVs)

A joint venture (JV) is a business arrangement where two or more parties collaborate to undertake a specific project or business activity, sharing resources, risks, and profits. JVs can be structured as:

- Contractual Agreements: Where parties collaborate without forming a separate legal entity.

- Equity-Based Entities: Where parties create a new entity (e.g., LLC or corporation) to conduct the joint venture business.

Contractual Joint Ventures

Contractual JVs are the most prevalent type of arrangement I see in the field. These are specifically appropriate for short-term projects or property-specific collaborations. They are easier to set up, require fewer formalities, and allow flexibility in defining rights and duties. They do not form a new legal entity, which means each party retains its own legal identity and is individually liable.

Contractual Joint Ventures are a "weak coupling" model. While they may be convenient, even ideal for temporary alliances, they are much riskier in terms of enforcement, dispute resolution, and exit planning. Risks include unclear obligations, enforcement challenges, and potential liability if one party underperforms or defaults.

Legal Standing

- No separate legal entity exists, so any dispute is resolved under contract law.

- Disputes are between the original parties, who remain individually liable for their actions and obligations.

Potential Impacts

- Direct Liability: Each party is exposed to legal and financial liability if the other breaches the contract or causes harm.

- Weaker Enforcement: Ambiguities in the contract can lead to lengthy litigation and interpretation disputes.

- No Shielding: Parties are not insulated from each other's debts or misconduct.

- Reputational Harm: Disputes can strain business relationships and tarnish credibility.

- Exit Difficulty: If no clear exit or dispute resolution mechanism is in place, disentangling from the JV can be complex and costly.

Risk Amplifiers

- Poorly drafted contracts.

- Vague dispute resolution clauses.

- Differences in jurisdiction or governing law.

Entity-Based Joint Ventures

These ventures typically involve an LLC or corporation jointly owned by the parties. This provides clear governance structures, defined ownership and liability, and a separate legal personality, which can protect the parent companies. Many larger or higher-risk ventures opt for equity-based entities to mitigate risks by creating legal clarity, asset protection, and enforceability.

⚠️ If your partnership structure involves capital contributions from multiple individuals, particularly where those individuals are not active in management, you may be entering syndication territory. See Chapter 10: *Understanding Capital* for guidance on Regulation D offerings and SEC compliance boundaries.

Legal Standing

- Disputes often involve the entity itself, not just the partners.
- Governed by corporate law, operating agreements, bylaws, and shareholder agreements.

Potential Impacts

- Limited Liability: Disputes are generally contained within the entity, reducing risk to parent companies.

- Clearer Governance: Operating agreements typically specify dispute mechanisms (e.g., board votes, arbitration).

- Asset Protection: The entity structure helps isolate assets and liabilities.

- Exit and Buy-Outs: Formal procedures (e.g., buy-sell provisions) can ease withdrawal or dissolution.

- Increased Complexity: Disputes may trigger regulatory filings, board actions, or shareholder lawsuits.

Risk Amplifiers

- Unequal control or deadlocks in decision-making.

- Misalignment between shareholder expectations and business outcomes.

- Breaches of fiduciary duty by directors or managers.

Comparison Chart

Aspect	Contractual JV	Equity-Based JV
Legal Framework.	Contract Law.	Corporate/Entity Law.
Liability Exposure.	Direct and Personal.	Generally Limited to Entity.
Dispute Resolution.	Negotiation or litigation.	Governed by Operating/Shareholder Terms.
Asset Separation.	None.	Yes, via the entity.
Exit Complexity.	High (if poorly drafted).	Moderate to Low (if well-structured).

Participation Models

After you choose your model, contract or entity, you need to dial in the participation model. These elements are the functional mechanics and rules that your contract or entity operating agreements contain. They define how capital and contribution convert into returns, and how roles are compensated or limited.

Equity Participation Agreements

These agreements assign economic interest, often a share of profits or appreciation, to a party who may not hold formal control or title. Use these when a capital partner wants to share upside but remain operationally passive. Returns may be fixed, tiered, or contingent on performance. These types of arrangements are common in preferred equity and structured joint ventures. Think of it as "you keep control. I share the upside."

Silent Partner Agreements

Silent partners provide capital without operational input or voting rights, typically for a defined return or profit share. Legal documentation must make their passive status explicit to avoid unintentional securities liability. Silent partner constructs are used when a party wants reliable returns without responsibility. Think of it as "you write the check. I run the show."

If a participant contributes capital and expects profits but plays no active role, you may be offering a security. Always consult a qualified attorney before promising returns to passive investors.

Sweat Equity Agreements

Sweat equity is the most misunderstood and misrepresented form of participation in creative finance deals. It represents contribution in the form of services, labor, access, or operational capacity. If you are contributing sweat equity, insist on documentation that describes specific roles and deliverables, establishes how and when equity is earned or vested, and defines triggers for payout or conversion into ownership percentage. For example, "operator will earn 30% equity in the project upon completion of the rehab scope within the agreed budget and timeline." In absence of performance benchmarks and clarity on vesting, sweat equity is an invitation for disagreements.

As a licensed agent, you must exercise extreme caution when entering sweat equity arrangements. Acting as both an equity partner and licensed representative creates layered fiduciary obligations that may conflict. You must disclose all roles in writing, seek broker approval, and in many cases, refrain from dual agency. If compensation is not routed through your brokerage, you risk license violation. Treat these arrangements as you would any principal involvement with full transparency and legal review.

Each of these participation models activates different combinations of the CART levers: control, access to capital, risk allocation, and terms. Structuring equity effectively means selecting the right balance of those forces inside your deal. Partnership structures are not just legal configurations; they are vehicles for creative leverage. The most effective equity splits activate multiple levers of the CART framework. Control is defined contractually or by ownership class. Access to Capital is multiplied through pooled contributions. Risk is distributed by agreement and mitigated through default protocols. Terms are shaped in operating agreements that define roles, rewards, and remedies. Strategic partnership design is creative finance at the entity level.

Operating Agreements and Control Rights

All partnerships should be governed by a written operating agreement. This document defines control, decision-making rights, and the treatment of major events. It must address the following questions:

- Who can sign contracts?
- Who can access capital accounts?
- How are profits distributed?
- What happens if one party wants to exit or defaults?
- How are disputes resolved?

You must address these issues whether you are forming an entity or using a contractual arrangement. A common oversight among agents who partner with investors is failing to formalize their role. You must ensure that your operating agreement does not blur your license obligations with partnership participation. Disclosure is essential.

Licensee-Specific Risks

When you act as both agent and investor, or when you receive an equity position in lieu of commission, you must:

- Provide written disclose of your license status to all parties.
- Clarify whether you are acting as an agent, a principal, or both.
- Avoid dual agency unless permitted and fully disclosed under your state law.
- Never collect undisclosed compensation or assignment fees.

Failing to properly define your role can lead to license suspension or revocation.

Compliance and Entity Selection

Not all equity structures are created equal. Some trigger securities registration, others expose you to unnecessary liability. You must choose the right entity structure:

- Limited Liability Corporation (LLC): Most common for JVs; flexible and scalable.

- Limited Partnership (LP): Often used when general and limited partners have distinct roles.

- Tenants in Common (TIC): An ownership designation only but used for shared title in multi-owner deals.

What is an Operating Agreement?

An Operating Agreement is a legal document that outlines the ownership structure, member roles, governance rules, and operational procedures of a Limited Liability Company (LLC). While not always legally required depending on the state, it is critical for defining internal rules, preventing disputes, and protecting limited liability status. For multi-member LLCs or equity-based joint ventures, it serves as the "constitution" of the business, setting expectations, rights, and responsibilities.

Must-Have Elements of a Comprehensive Operating Agreement

The following elements should be included in every operating agreement as best practice, but you may need to add provisions to cover aspects of your business arrangements that are unique. I recommend using legal counsel to assist you with writing provisions for your specific requirements.

Basic Company Information
- Name of the LLC.

- Principal business address.

- Registered agent name and address.

- Formation date and state of organization.

- Purpose of the LLC (can be broad or specific).

Member Information

- Names and addresses of members.

- Initial capital contributions (cash, property, or services).

- Ownership percentages (and how they're determined).

Management Structure

- Specify whether the LLC is:

- Member-managed (all members run the business).

- Manager-managed (delegated to one or more managers).

- Duties and powers of managers.

- Appointment and removal procedures.

Voting Rights and Procedures

- Voting power based on ownership or one-member-one-vote.

- Matters requiring unanimous vs. majority approval.

- Deadlock resolution mechanisms.

Profit and Loss Allocation

- How profits and losses will be divided.

- Distribution schedules (e.g., quarterly, annually).

Meetings and Record-Keeping

- Requirements for meetings (if any).

- Notice provisions, quorum rules.
- Maintenance of records and financial statements.

Fiduciary Duties and Liability

- Define duties of loyalty and care.
- Indemnification clauses for members or managers.
- Limitations of liability, if legally allowed.

Banking and Fiscal Matters

- Designation of fiscal year.
- Procedures for opening bank accounts.
- Tax classification (e.g., partnership, corporation, disregarded entity).

Transfers of Interest

- Restrictions on transfers (right of first refusal, buy-sell rules).
- Admission of new members.
- Death, disability, or bankruptcy of a member.

Dispute Resolution

- Preferred methods (mediation, arbitration, court).
- Jurisdiction and governing law.
- Deadlock-breaking provisions for 50/50 ventures.

Dissolution and Winding Up

- Events triggering dissolution.
- Winding-up procedures.
- Distribution of remaining assets.

Miscellaneous Provisions

- Amendment procedures.

- Entire agreement clause.

- Severability, waiver, and notice provisions.

When Not to Partner

Not every deal needs a partner. Use caution when roles are undefined or overlap, or exit plans are unclear. Do not engage with a partner who lacks experience but expects equal returns. If the project is too small to justify shared returns, know your worth. Exit planning is entry planning. Know how you will separate before you agree to unite.

Conclusion: Build Smart, Not Fast

Partnerships create opportunity, but only when built on structure. As a licensed agent or broker operating in creative finance, your duty is to align entrepreneurial opportunity with ethical and compliant practices. Do not rely on informal agreements or verbal promises. Document everything. Protect your license, protect your capital, and protect your partners by being the one who brings professionalism to the table. Creative partnerships should never feel casual. Done properly, they become the highest-leverage tool in your creative finance toolbox.

Chapter 12:
Working with Investors

Understanding creative financing allows you to penetrate the investor community and increase the number of closings in the opportunity stream you are already generating and managing. It increases your yield. The world of creative finance is populated with investors. If you endeavor to become a Master of Creative Finance, you are committing yourself to working with the investor community.

The upside of working with investors is that they are evergreen clients with whom you may engage in ten or more transactions per year. If you track your lead generation efforts and costs and understand your client acquisition cost, you know that finding the buyers and sellers who purchase or sell a home once every five or ten years requires a significant investment in time and dollars. Investors, on the other hand, bring capital, repeat transactions, and access to deals that fall outside traditional channels. The downside, if you think of it that way, they also demand discounts and they also bring risk.

Investor clients are not like primary homebuyers. Except when they are buying or selling their own primary home, they do not shop with emotion. They shop with metrics, and they are hungry for high-leverage deals. They do not ask if the kitchen is bright. They ask what the exit strategy is. In this chapter, I describe how to identify different investor profiles, structure clean relationships, package deals in investor-ready formats, and build a durable investor practice that allows you to create a steady revenue stream beyond one-time closings. Understand that you must define your role clearly and structure your engagements properly, or you risk your license, your reputation, and your ability to scale.

A Mindset and Possible Association Shift

You have probably heard the line that if you are an agent acting outside your local area, you are not acting competently. That statement assumes that most of the time you are assisting families find right-fit homes and neighborhoods and counseling newcomers to the community. At this point AI can provide much of what the primary homebuyer needs for community insight. Your personal insights may be unique, but not as vital as they were twenty or even ten years ago.

Your investor clients, on the other hand, tend to have more expansive geofencing. Many investors have multi-state portfolio goals while others focus on specific regions in specific states. The only geofence your license conveys are state borders. Licensed in multiple states? Good on you. More opportunities! Multi-state investors open the door to building a referral revenue stream in your business.

When it comes to working with investors, the truth about geographic competency is that the local realtor association structure writ large creates obstacles to your access to local knowledge and disclosures that you need to provide competent transaction services across county lines. This means that you need to research real estate transfer requirements for transfer taxes, specific local area disclosures, local inspections, retrofit requirements, and the like on your own, or opt to join additional associations.

If you choose to focus on investors, be prepared to sustain multiple MLS subscriptions and be prepared for a significant amount of frustration exploring the data-share maze to determine what combination of MLS subscriptions work best for you. For me, my local MLS is a subset of what I get from an association 120 miles away. While it is nice to have relationships with other local agents, it ends up being a costly luxury for me.

Finally, on this topic, you may need to reconsider your broker affiliation to realize your potential in the investor market. The footprint of your agency determines the access you have to MLS data and the resource pool of other agents that you can access for easy collaboration. Rehoming yourself may be the only solution to expanding your reach and increasing the type of transactions for which you are able to provide services.

Understanding Investor Profiles

Investor profiles vary widely along with the property types and outcomes they seek. If you treat every investor the same, you will serve none of them well. Your job is not to guess what they need. Your job is to ask, categorize, and match deals to decision styles and capital strategies. Before I parse individual investor types, it is important that you understand real estate wholesaling because wholesaling is as integral to the zeitgeist of the investor culture as thread is to fabric.

Wholesalers

Wholesaling real estate is the acquisition and sale of contracts, not properties. Wholesalers get discounted properties under contract and assign the contracts to third parties for a fee. While wholesaling is not an investment strategy per se, it is an onramp to investing. It is important that you understand that all the real estate investment gurus who have training programs and mentorships recommend wholesaling as a means of generating revenue for newbies who do not have funding. Not only does this process teach people how to understand real estate, but it also teaches them how to prospect for deals.

Some of my best clients are wholesalers. That said, as an agent you should know that wholesalers who know what they are doing are eating your lunch because many of them are simply out working you. Wholesalers look for deals both on and off the market. If you are a residential listing agent who has received a letter of intent (LOI) for your listing, chances are you are dealing with a wholesaler despite the fact that they are presenting themselves as buyers.

Some of you reading this might be asking yourself "how is this legal?" In some states it is not. For instance, South Carolina made it illegal for both licensed and unlicensed individuals effective in 2024. Some states impose limits on the number of transactions an unlicensed wholesaler may complete in a twelve-month period such as California (7), Michigan (5) and Illinois (1). Many more states require a real estate license such as North Carolina, Oklahoma and Maryland to name just a few.

I recommend partnering with ethical wholesalers whenever it makes sense. Even wholesalers can benefit from partnerships with agents. Your license can bridge the gap between state limitations and legally completing more transactions for a wholesaler by providing them with transactional services. Be careful not to engage in fee splitting or mixing compensation. When I represent a wholesaler, the contract between us is subject to assignment along with the purchase agreement. As you venture into the investor world and start engaging at the community level you are going to meet many wholesalers. Some of the largest wholesalers operate as brokerages, some are nationally franchised. You quickly learn that you need all the friends you can get in the industry.

Investor Archetypes

There are two primary categories of investors, portfolio investors (aka Buy-and-Hold) and resellers (aka Fix-and-Flip and developers). Buy-and-Hold Investors seek long-term cash flow, depreciation benefits, and equity growth. They often purchase single-family rentals or small multifamily properties. Their focus is on yield, durability of rent, and low tenant turnover. They respond well to seller financing, master lease options, and installment sale contracts. Portfolio investors are focused on building generational wealth.

Fix-and-Flip and developer investors prioritize margin and, for smaller projects, speed. They are interested in purchase price, repair costs and building costs, and resale value. Time is capital. They may be backed by hard money lenders or private partners, or they may use their own cash. Deals with clear comps, reasonable timelines and favorable repair scopes interest fix and flippers the most. Resellers are focused on generating current income. Developers have longer payback goals.

These investor types operate at various scales from mom-and-pop to large-scale institutional investors from hedge funds to real estate investment trusts (REITs). Institutional investors tend to internalize brokerage services so you will likely bring the most value to smaller investors.

What is an Exit Strategy?

A simple answer to the question is what you do with the property after you buy it. Investors purchase properties, transform them by adding value, and then either place them into service to generate positive cashflow or resell them for a profit. The term *Exit Strategy* can be confusing because the word *exit* implies an ending but, in the investor-sphere, it also refers to a new beginning.

You can largely define investors by their exit strategies. You must understand the exit strategy an investor is pursuing to align with and serve their needs. Some investors are very focused on one exit strategy while others may be interested in multiple strategies. Investor exit strategies evolve over time as their net worth grows, their goals change. Someone who starts with single family rentals in specific types of neighborhoods after accumulating a couple hundred doors might decide to transition to large multi-family properties. If you want to grow with your clients, you need to keep up with them!

Popular Exit Strategies

Your opportunity horizon expands immensely when you begin to think beyond the primary homebuyer and single-family homes. Some of these have business components and may require you to speak with your broker before you engage. Many of these require you to level up your skills. A world of possibilities awaits.

Single family strategies (including condominiums):

- Fix and flip: There is an ongoing need for neighborhood renewal. Flippers help drive the gentrification process.

- BRRRR Method: A buy-and-hold strategy that starts with properties in need of renovation. BRRRR is an acronym for Buy-Reno-vate-Rent-Refinance-Repeat. Refinancing frees up cash for purchasing the next project.

- Single family rentals: A buy-and-hold strategy that starts with properties that may not require renovations or need only simple cosmetic changes. Always popular for rentals because they are easy to remarket to primary homebuyers.

- Small multi-family: An evergreen target for portfolio buyers, and very popular with house hackers, typically first-time buyers who intend to live in one of the units.

- Senior living: Assisted living is in high demand as baby boomers reach their later years. Additional knowledge acquisition required.

- Low-income housing: Some investors specialize in section 8 housing and are always looking to expand their portfolio. Development opportunities exist at a much larger scale.

- Co-living: An emerging market trend that works to satisfy both low-income housing in urban areas and high-end experiential housing for remote working communities.

- Mid-term rentals: Serving the needs of travel workers and temporary housing for people displaced by housing loss.

- Vacation rentals: While the frenzy to get into this market has passed, it remains a solid investment strategy for investors who know how to operate them.

Other asset classes (businesses with real estate)

- Mobile home parks: Renting dirt provides real estate income without the need to fix toilets.

- RV parks: These can be very basic to full-on resorts with multiple revenue streams.

- Boutique Motels: These are an extension of the short-term vacation rental trend that do not run headlong into STR restrictions.

- Large multi-family: A favored asset class for investors who raise capital in funds or who have larger portfolios.

- Office to apartments conversions: A high opportunity market especially in urban areas.

The above list is merely a sampling. Once you begin to engage with investor communities you will discover that there are endless possibilities because investors are always creating new trends.

Learning the Language and New Skills

You are not going to attract investor clients because of your depth of knowledge in local school systems but you will impress them with your ability to underwrite an investment, your deep knowledge of market trends, and by delivering meaningful comps to assist them with their buy decisions. A fix-and-flip or BRRRR investor will love you for your ability to estimate repairs and after repair value (ARV). Similarly, your buy-and-hold investors will find you invaluable if you can model cashflow and acquisition costs for them accurately. Investors are professional capital deployers. Your goal is to become useful to them.

What is a Buy Box?

A buy box is investor lingo for a definition of their acquisition target(s). These may be broad and encompass multiple geographies or be hyper targeted to specific cities and neighborhoods. An example of a buy box:

- Single Family Co-living.

- 3/2 or more.

- Min 1800 sq. ft.

- Light rehab.

- Houston or Dallas.

Underwriting Deals

There are multiple components to underwriting real estate investment deals. Cashflow is the determining factor for buy-and-hold exit strategies. To determine cashflow subtract expenses from income.

- Revenue: Rents and other income.

- Base Costs: Principal, interest, taxes, and insurance (PITI).

- Additional Costs: SOLAR, Utilities, HOA, Maintenance and the amount you allocate for reserves (CAPEX) typically a percentage of revenue.

- If the investment includes transforming the property by remodeling or making other types of improvements to its resale or revenue potential, you need to model project costs.

- Repairs and improvements: Materials and labor.

- Holding Costs: Base costs plus additional costs less any preserved revenue such as rents from units not taken out of service.

- If you are underwriting a BRRRR method or fix-and-flip, understanding carrying costs and cashflow is critical. Most hard money lenders release construction funds based on completion milestones, which means that the investor must front the money to pay for materials and labor and monthly carrying costs before they are able to draw down their construction funds. The impact is that an investor must have enough cash on hand to cover:

- Downpayment.

- Closing costs including loan fees and points.

- Carry costs including PITI, utilities, permits and inspections.

- Funds to cover cash outlays until draws begin funding.

I include an underwriting spreadsheet in the book download. Note that it is in the form of a Google Sheet so you will need to use the provided link and make a copy of it. There is a link to a how-to use video embedded in the sheet.

My intent here is not to take a deep dive into underwriting, rather it is to put you on notice that you need to learn this skill for each asset type and exit strategy that you want to support. The better you are at these basic skills, the more valuable you are to your investor clients.

Level Up Your Comping Skills

While underwriting deals is a number-crunching exercise, comping for investors is as much art as it is a numbers game. The goals of this exercise vary for investor types. Buy-and-hold investors want to make sure that they aren't overpaying. Fix-and-flip buyers are comping for potential in a what-if exercise to determine the finish levels and design aesthetics they need to apply to maximize the value. Both may need your support with convincing lenders of current and future value.

Comping for future value is a significant departure from comping for current value. To do this you are looking for an exemplar(s) to establish maximum future value (ARV) usually for a flipper. Similar to comping for current value, you try to adhere to the standard rules of staying within a subdivision and finding a model match, but the difference is you need to be able to visualize the added value that the proposed repairs and finish levels will bring to your subject property.

How to Find Investor Clients

You have content coming at you by the minute from marketing gurus and referral companies promising to unlock the secrets of explosive growth, so I assume that you know what good marketing habits are, whether you have a well-established discipline or not. That is on you. Most of the principles are the same only the audience changes.

The most effective way to find clients is to engage in community activities. Rather than focusing on local school organizations, chambers of commerce, and religious groups, you need to direct your attention to investor communities. The quickest way to get started is using social media to find them. Search Facebook groups. LinkedIn groups, and explore Bigger Pockets forums to find both national, regional and local communities of investors.

Even the smallest communities have local real estate investment associations (REIAs). These are a good place to start when you want to expand your local networking efforts. Social media, Facebook in particular, is a good place to find them. Select groups in Facebook and enter "real estate investment" in the search. You will be overwhelmed with results. Focus on the groups with either a regional focus that interests you or ones with large memberships.

You should explore Creative Real Estate with Pace Morby, and Astro Flipping with Jamil Damji. There are public and private versions of each of these. I recommend joining Pace Morby's Sub To private community. The price of admission may seem high, but I can assure you that it is well worth the investment. Keep in mind that you only get out of a group what you invest in it.

If you want to find flippers, use a property data service such as one you might obtain for free from your favorite title company or a paid commercial service to find properties that were purchased and resold in less than a year. Use skip tracing services or other means to find the contact information for the principals. Analyze the track record of your flipper to determine their preferred product types and location choices. Impress them with the fact that you studied their preferences and bring them potential opportunities on your first call to demonstrate your potential value.

Conclusion: Building an Investor Practice

A single investor client can produce five transactions per year, or fifty. What matters is how you nurture the relationship. Always lead with value. Keep in mind that these are evergreen relationships and that a handful of investor clients can fill your dance card. Once you establish and grow these relationships, you will not have to spend an enormous amount of your time prospecting for new clients like you do in the retail real estate world.

Chapter 13:
Buyer, Seller, and Agent Conversations

Every meaningful conversation begins with psychology. No deal structure succeeds unless it resonates with emotional logic, not just the math. In this chapter I provide you with the mindset, sequencing, and language needed to turn creative concepts into conversational alignment.

The core obstacle you face with all audiences is that many if not most of the people to whom you speak about creative strategies have never heard of these constructs. Even the most experienced brokers and agents are only vaguely aware of how alternative financing arrangements work and can benefit their clients. People generally fear what they do not know. Therein lies the challenge.

Listing Agent to Seller Conversations

Most agents approach sellers with presentations. That is what you have been taught to do. It is the industry standard. You prepare a comparative marketing analysis (CMA), and you pitch your unique marketing prowess and advantages using paper and electronic assets.

Agents who understand creative financing go a step further by investigating the seller's existing loans and liens. By doing this, you learn in advance which creative strategies are potentially available to accelerate the sales process and if there are options for the seller to expand their revenue from the sale. That is a monumental differentiator!

I take a different approach to the listing meeting. Yes, I arrive with historic market data in hand to support valuation discussions, but I do not present. Instead, I conduct a real estate therapy session. While others "pitch," my strategy is to achieve alignment.

Sellers are not numbers on a spreadsheet. They are human beings navigating fear, timing pressure, uncertainty, and identity. You must see the problem through their eyes:

- Are they facing a shortfall or foreclosure?
- Do they need to preserve pride while exiting a failed plan?
- Are they stuck on price because they are anchored to yesterday's market?

The real obstacle is not the terms. It is the fear of regret. As we all do, sellers fear making a decision today that looks foolish six months from now. They fear giving up certainty for creativity. They fear loss of control.

Creative conversations with sellers must begin with empathy, not options. Before presenting structure, ask questions that reveal the seller's frame of mind.

- What worries you most about this process?
- If I could remove one pain point, what would it be?
- Are you looking for top price, fast timeline, or peace of mind?

The Seller's Timeline and Trade-Offs

Sellers live on a timeline. The key to creative structure is helping them see how delayed gratification can create greater certainty and often a higher net. This is especially relevant in:

- Seller financing: where payments over time create income and defer taxes.
- Lease options: where a tenant-buyer proves themselves before purchase.
- Subject-To and wraps: where speed beats price.

Talking Points for Sellers

Introduce this framing directly: "Would you be open to getting more money overall, even if it comes in installments rather than a lump sum?"

Or: "If I could show you how to get your full asking price without sitting on the market, would you be open to a different structure?"

The transition from listening to presenting is delicate. You must ask for permission:

"Would it be okay if I shared a few strategies other sellers in your position have used to get better outcomes?"

Then lead with metaphors:

"It is like selling the payments, not just the property."

"Imagine you become the bank, you keep control, and the buyer pays you over time."

Do not use jargon. Avoid terms like wrap, Subject-To, or option until the seller understands the function. Know in advance which strategies are doable.

Unrepresented Sellers

Most agents rarely speak with unrepresented sellers outside the context of a listing pitch. When you work with wholesalers who pursue Subject-To or other creative strategies, it becomes a common occurrence. Wholesalers are more likely to use an agent to close a creative sale than a cash deal. When you do find yourself working with a wholesaler on a cash deal, it is more likely than not that the wholesaler is seeking to shelter the transaction with your license.

The majority of the creative deals you encounter with unrepresented sellers are distressed properties. If they are not already in the pre-foreclosure process (notice of default or notice of sale) they are often on that track.

You may be tempted to dive into dual agency in these situations, but I caution against it. The majority of lawsuits in real estate transactions derive from dual agnecy deals. The risk is amplified when you include pre-foreclosure circumstances and creative deal structures. Beyond that, these sellers are rarely able to sustain increased costs in the transaction.

Talking Points for Unrepresented Sellers

Clearly explain the agency relationship: "I owe my highest duty and loyalty to the buyer with whom I have a fiduciary relationship."

Next, explain your duties to the seller. "I owe you a duty to disclose all material facts. The buyer brought me into the transaction to make certain that you are protected in the transaction."

Ensure that the seller is aware that the buyer intends to assign the contract to a different buyer.

Do not work with wholesalers who are not comfortable with disclosing their intent to assign the contract or who wish to hide their profit in the deal. These are material facts and must be fully disclosed.

Best Practices

Most wholesalers use non-standard contracts. Insist on using your state or brokerage standard. You can substitute a new contract using an amendment that states the original contract is replaced in its entirety with the new contract. After replacing the original contract proceed with all standard disclosures and advisories required by your state and brokerage using standard forms. Numerous states, including California, require statutory cancellation periods in contracts once a notice of default is served. If your wholesaler client is unaware of these statutory requirements, you are protecting their interest by retrofitting compliance into their contractual process.

Talking to Agents or Brokers

Conversations with other agents and brokers can be very difficult when they are unfamiliar with creative strategies. Many of these conversations center around the legality of Subject-To transactions, which I covered in Chapter 5. For the purposes of this discussion, you need to understand the actual language of the due-on-sale provision.

Sample Due on Sale Provision

> **Transfer of the Property or a Beneficial Interest in Borrower.** As used in this section, "Interest in the Property" means any legal or beneficial interest in the Property, including but not limited to, those beneficial interests transferred in a bond for deed, contract for deed, installment sales contract or escrow agreement, the intent of which is the transfer of title by Borrower at a future date to a purchaser.
>
> If all or any part of the Property or any interest in the Property is sold or transferred (or if Borrower is not a natural persona and a beneficial interest in Borrower is sold or transferred) without Lender's prior written consent, lender may require immediate payment in full of all sums secured by the Security Instrument. However, this option shall not be exercised by Lender if such exercise is prohibited by Applicable Law.
>
> If Lender exercises this option, Lender shall give Borrower notice of acceleration. The notice shall provide a period of not less than 30 days from the date the notice is given in accordance with Section XX within which Borrower must pay all sums secured by the Security Instrument. If Borrower fails to pay these sums prior to the expiration of this period,

Lender may invoke any remedies permitted by this Security Instrument without further notice or demand on Borrower.

Talking Points for the Due on Sale Clause

Notice the specific language used in the second paragraph, "lender may require immediate payment." These provisions use the word "may," rather than "shall."

While the language in most modern versions of due-on-sale provisions are inclusive of executory contract structures, the lenders do not (cannot) preclude leases or options. A carefully structured lease agreement with a separate option agreement is a workable fallback solution. This is why I include this in the purchase agreement.

Talking Points for Agent Conversations

Another way to get agents to warm up to creative solutions is to engage with them on business challenges from the perspective of a sympathetic, agent-to-agent conversation.

"Are you satisfied with your production in recent years?"

"Do you want to learn how other agents are closing more deals?"

You can offer to let the other agent in on the "secret" to closing more deals using creative financing structures. Share your own success stories. Become a friend, not a sparring partner.

"Are you aware of the existing loans and liens on your listings? Did you know that these may present opportunities to accelerate your sale? Would you like to learn more about these possibilities?"

Conclusion

Metaphorically, your life is a continuous flow of communication. Each conversation contributes to the overall narrative of your experience and influences who you become. Recognizing the impact of your interactions with buyers, sellers, agents and other professionals is key to influencing outcomes. Be the person who actively cultivates positive interactions. Lead with empathy and authenticity to achieve success.

Glossary of Terms

Term	Definition
Access to Capital	The ability to obtain funds for real estate transactions through sources other than traditional banks, including seller financing, private money, crowdfunding, or hypothecation. A key lever in structuring creative deals.
Accredited Investor	An individual or entity that meets financial thresholds set by securities regulators, allowing participation in certain private placements and syndications.
Acquisition Funnel	A visual or strategic model used to describe the flow of property leads from initial contact to final acquisition. The LPO Method relies on a consistent funnel to sustain deal volume.
Agency	A fiduciary relationship in which a licensed real estate professional acts on behalf of a buyer or seller in a transaction. Creative finance increases the complexity and risk of agency, particularly when roles blur.
AI (Artificial Intelligence)	A class of technologies that simulate human intelligence. In real estate, AI tools can perform tasks such as valuation modeling, listing generation, and transaction assistance, potentially replacing certain agent functions.

Term	Definition
All-Inclusive Trust Deed (AITD)	Abbreviation for All-Inclusive Trust Deed. A financing instrument where the seller carries a note that includes the balance of any existing mortgage, effectively wrapping the underlying loan.
Amortization	The process of spreading loan payments over time, typically in regular installments, that cover both principal and interest. Creative terms may include non-standard amortization.
Amortization Schedule	A table outlining periodic loan payments, showing amounts allocated to principal and interest over time. Used to structure consistent repayment in installment contracts.
Amortized Note	A promissory note structured to repay both principal and interest over time, typically in equal installments. Standardized repayment schedule provides predictability.
Arrearage	The total past-due amounts owed on a mortgage loan, including missed principal, interest, taxes, and insurance payments. Often cured by the buyer in subject-to deals to bring the loan current.
Assignment Right	The legal ability to transfer one's interest in a contract, lease, or option agreement to another party.

Term	Definition
Balloon Note	A loan structure that requires a large payment at the end of the term after smaller periodic payments. Used to defer full repayment while maximizing early affordability.
Balloon Payment	A large, lump-sum payment due at the end of a loan term, following smaller periodic payments. Often used in seller financing to defer full payoff.
Broker	A licensed real estate professional authorized to supervise agents and accept liability for transactions. Brokers determine which creative strategies agents may implement under their license.
Brokerage	The legal entity that employs or contracts with real estate agents. Brokerages set policy, manage risk, and provide resources or restrictions for creative finance engagements.
Cancellation Rate	The percentage of real estate purchase agreements that are initiated but subsequently canceled before closing. A high cancellation rate indicates instability in market transactions.
Capital Call	A formal request made by a sponsor or fund manager to investors, asking them to provide committed capital to finance a deal or meet funding obligations.
Capital Contribution	The initial or ongoing financial input made by a partner or member into a joint venture or entity, typically in the form of cash, services, or assets.

Term	Definition
Capital Deployment	The strategic allocation of investment capital into real estate assets, projects, or loans with the intent of generating returns.
Capital Stack	The layered combination of capital sources in a transaction, including equity, debt, and subordinated financing. Understanding stack order is critical in creative deal design.
CART	An acronym for the Four levers of creative finance: Control, Access to Capital, Risk Allocation, and Terms. A structural framework for designing and analyzing creative transactions.
Cash-on-Cash Return	A financial metric comparing the annual pre-tax cash flow received from an investment to the total cash invested. Often used to evaluate leveraged deals.
Compliance	Adherence to applicable laws, regulations, brokerage policies, and ethical standards in a real estate transaction. In creative finance, compliance ensures innovation does not breach legal boundaries.
Contract for Deed	A financing arrangement where the seller retains legal title while the buyer makes installment payments. Title transfers only after all payments are completed. See also Installment Sale, Land Contract.
Contractual Joint Venture (CJV)	A short-term business collaboration governed solely by a written agreement. CJVs do not involve creating a new legal entity.

Term	Definition
Control	The ability to direct decisions and outcomes related to a property, such as use, improvements, or resale, even without full legal ownership. Commonly achieved via lease-options or equitable interests.
Creative Deal	A real estate transaction structured using non-traditional terms or instruments to achieve strategic objectives. Distinguished by adaptability across the CART levers.
Creative Finance	A strategic approach to structuring real estate transactions using non-traditional methods such as seller financing, lease options, or subject-to arrangements. It prioritizes problem-solving and deal preservation over institutional loan qualification.
Cross-Collateralization	A financing arrangement in which one loan is secured by multiple properties or assets. In wraparound structures, this can increase leverage but complicates foreclosure remedies.
Deal Flow	The volume and quality of real estate transactions entering the pipeline. Strong deal flow is essential for consistent closings under the LPO framework.
Deal Presentation	A structured summary of a proposed investment, including terms, financials, and risk factors. Used to pitch opportunities to prospective investors.

Term	Definition
Deal Structure	The specific configuration of terms, roles, obligations, and instruments used to complete a real estate transaction. In creative finance, structure is the key determinant of viability.
Debt Partner	An investor who contributes capital in the form of a loan to the deal and expects repayment with interest. Holds no ownership rights.
Debt Service	The total amount required to cover loan payments, including principal and interest, over a given period. Affects overall deal viability.
Deed of Trust	A security instrument in which a borrower conveys title to a neutral trustee to hold on behalf of a lender until the debt is repaid. Common in western states.
Default Cure	The process of resolving a loan default by paying past-due amounts, penalties, or fees to reinstate the loan and stop foreclosure proceedings.
Default Provision	A clause that outlines the consequences and remedies if the buyer fails to comply with the payment terms. May include forfeiture or reinstatement rights.
Default Remedy	The course of action outlined in a financing agreement if a borrower fails to meet obligations. May include foreclosure, forfeiture, or acceleration of debt.

Term	Definition
Default Risk	The probability that a borrower will fail to meet the terms of the loan, triggering remedies such as foreclosure. Higher in wraparound deals due to informal servicing or subordinate position.
Deferred Capital Gains	A tax strategy where gains on real estate are not immediately taxed due to installment sale structuring. Applies to certain seller-financed transactions.
Disclosure	The act of making all material facts known to clients and counterparties in a transaction. Creative deals require expanded, explicit disclosures to ensure informed consent.
Disclosure Addendum	A supplementary document in a subject-to transaction disclosing the presence of an existing loan, risks associated with the due-on-sale clause, and the parties' obligations.
Disclosure Statement	A written document that provides all material facts and risks related to a transaction. Required in wraparound deals to ensure informed consent by all parties.
Downpayment	The initial lump sum paid by a buyer at closing. Reduces loan principal and reflects buyer commitment.
Due Diligence Period	The timeframe granted to the buyer or optionee to inspect the property, verify terms, and evaluate feasibility before full commitment. Often negotiated in lease-option structures.

Term	Definition
Due-on-Sale Clause	A mortgage provision granting the lender the right but not obligation to demand full repayment if ownership transfers without their consent. Often triggered in subject-to transactions.
Due-on-Sale Risk	The potential for the existing lender to call the full loan due if title or equitable interest transfers, even in indirect arrangements such as contracts for deed.
Entity-Based Joint Venture (EBJV)	A formal partnership structured through a legal entity, typically an LLC, offering centralized management and limited liability protection.
Equitable Interest	A legal interest in property that conveys the right to use, benefit from, or eventually acquire ownership of real estate, even when legal title remains with the seller. Often arises in installment contracts or lease-options.
Equity Multiple	A financial metric representing total return on invested capital. Calculated as total distributions divided by total capital invested.
Equity Participation Agreement	A contract granting a party an ownership interest in a venture in exchange for capital, services, or other contributions.
Equity Partner	An investor who provides capital in exchange for ownership interest in a deal. Shares in profits and losses.

Term	Definition
Equity Share	The portion of ownership and associated profit rights allocated to an investor or party in a real estate transaction.
Escrow	A neutral third party that holds funds, documents, or instructions until all contractual obligations are met. In creative deals, escrow must be familiar with non-traditional instruments.
Escrow Holdback	A portion of funds withheld in escrow post-closing to cover contingent obligations, such as loan reinstatement or repair completion. Helps protect the buyer or seller.
Escrow Instructions	Written directives to the escrow company outlining the terms, documents, and disbursements required to close the transaction. In subject-to deals, these must address existing loan handling.
Existing Loan	The mortgage already encumbering the property at the time of sale. In subject-to transactions, the buyer agrees to take title while leaving this loan in place.
Exit Strategy	The planned method for disposing of or profiting from a property after acquisition, such as resale, refinance, or rental. Selected in coordination with financing and control strategy.
Exit Timeline	The projected period within which an investment is expected to mature, refinance, or liquidate, returning capital and profits to investors.

Term	Definition
Fiduciary	A person or institution with a legal and ethical obligation to act in the best interests of another party. Real estate licensees are fiduciaries when representing clients.
Fiduciary Duty	A legal obligation to act in the best interest of another party, particularly relevant for licensees in partnership scenarios.
First Position	A lien with senior priority over all others. Typically, the original mortgage or the seller note if there is no pre-existing debt.
Foreclosure Rights	The legal remedies available to a lienholder in the event of borrower default. In wraps, both senior and junior lienholders may have separate and conflicting rights.
Forfeiture Clause	A provision that allows the seller to cancel the contract and retain payments made if the buyer defaults. Unique to installment land contracts.
Free and Clear	Describes a property unencumbered by debt or liens. Seller-financing is most flexible when properties are free and clear.
Full Wrap	A wraparound mortgage that covers the entire balance of an existing underlying loan, with the seller financing the full purchase price.
General Partner	The active manager in a syndication or joint venture who oversees operations and decision-making. May also contribute capital and receive a management fee or promote.

Term	Definition
Graduated Payments	A repayment structure where payments increase over time, aligning with anticipated income growth or investment returns. Enhances affordability and flexibility in deal structuring.
Hard Money	Asset-based lending typically provided by private individuals or funds. Characterized by short terms, higher interest rates, and minimal underwriting.
Hypothecation	The use of a promissory note or other asset from one deal as collateral for another. A technique for unlocking capital without liquidating equity.
Installment Sale	Another term for Contract for Deed. A sale where the buyer pays the purchase price over time in scheduled payments. Allows tax deferral and flexibility in deal structuring.
Interest Rate	The cost of borrowing money, expressed as a percentage of the principal. May be fixed or adjustable in contract for deed structures.
Interest Spread	The difference between the interest rate of the wraparound note and the underlying mortgage. This spread generates profit for the seller or investor.
Interest-Only	A loan arrangement in which the borrower pays only the interest for a specified period, with principal due later or at maturity. Used to increase affordability.

Term	Definition
Investor Agreement	A legal contract that defines the rights, roles, and responsibilities of an investor in a real estate transaction or fund.
Investor Buyer	A party who purchases real estate with the intent to generate income, equity, or both, rather than to occupy the property as a primary residence.
Investor Pitch Deck	A presentation document outlining the investment opportunity, team, market, and projected returns. Used to secure interest from potential investors.
Investor Portal	A digital platform through which investors can access documents, performance updates, and communication from the sponsor or syndicator.
Investor Profile	A summary of an investor's financial background, goals, and risk tolerance. Used to match deals to appropriate investor types.
Investor Qualification	The process of verifying that an investor meets regulatory and strategic criteria to participate in a given offering.
Investor Update	A periodic communication sent to investors detailing project performance, financials, and material developments.
Joint Venture	A business arrangement in which two or more parties collaborate on a single project or investment while retaining distinct ownership and roles.

Term	Definition
Junior Lien	A lien that is subordinate in priority to another. In wraps, the seller's new note is typically a junior lien to the existing mortgage.
Land Contract	Another term for Contract for Deed. Refers to the buyer's payment over time in exchange for future delivery of legal title.
Lease Option	A two-part agreement granting the tenant the right, but not obligation, to purchase the property at pre-agreed terms while leasing it. Offers control without immediate financing.
Lease Purchase	A hybrid structure where the tenant agrees to lease the property and is contractually obligated to purchase at the end of the lease term. Distinguished from lease-option by its enforceability.
Lease Term	The duration of the lease agreement. Its expiration may coincide with, or trigger, option execution in lease-option or lease-purchase contracts.
Legacy Financing	An existing mortgage or financial arrangement carried over from a prior transaction, typically referenced in subject-to or wraparound structures to preserve favorable terms.
Legal Title	The formal ownership of property recognized by the state. In a contract for deed, this remains with the seller until full performance by the buyer.

Term	Definition
Lien Priority	The order in which liens are paid off in foreclosure. Wraparound lenders typically hold subordinate positions, increasing their risk.
Limited Partner	A passive investor in a partnership who provides capital but does not participate in management. Liability is limited to the amount invested.
Loan Reinstatement	The act of restoring a delinquent loan to current status by paying the full arrearage, fees, and penalties due. Often a prerequisite in subject-to closings.
Loan Servicer	An entity or individual responsible for collecting payments, managing records, and handling disbursements in a loan. Often engaged in wraparound structures for neutrality.
Loan Servicing	The management of loan payments, recordkeeping, and communication with the lender. May be handled by a third-party servicer or informally by buyer and seller.
Locked-In Rate	A fixed mortgage interest rate secured by a borrower under a prior loan agreement. These rates often become assets in creative financing when newer rates are substantially higher.

Term	Definition
LPO	Acronym for Lease-Purchase-Option method. A creative strategy using three agreements that allows an investor to lease a property and improve it with an option to purchase it in the future. Offers control, cashflow, and potential equity gain without immediate financing.
LPO Method	A stepwise creative financing strategy involving a lease, a purchase agreement, and an option contract. Used to secure control and profit from a property while deferring ownership and financing.
Master Lease	A lease in which the lessee obtains control over the property and may sublease to others. Used in multifamily, commercial, or investment strategies for property control without ownership.
Mortgage	A legal instrument in which real property is pledged as security for a loan. Creates a lien in favor of the lender. More common in eastern states.
Mortgage Originator	An individual or institution that initiates and processes mortgage loans. Some seller-financing structures may trigger originator licensing requirements depending on state laws.
Mortgage Rate Differential	The gap between a seller's existing mortgage rate and current market rates. In creative finance, this spread creates leverage and incentive for non-traditional deal structures.

Term	Definition
Non-Assumable Loan	A mortgage that contractually prohibits another party from formally taking over the loan. Subject-to structures bypass formal assumption while maintaining legal, not contractual, compliance.
Non-Refundable Fee	A payment made upfront that is not returned if the buyer or optionee fails to execute the purchase. Typically applies to option fees or consideration.
Note	A written, legally binding promise to repay a debt under specific terms. The core evidence of indebtedness in seller-financed transactions.
Note Investor	A party who purchases promissory notes, often at a discount, to collect interest or enforce the debt. Can be active or passive.
Operating Agreement	A legal document governing an LLC's internal operations, defining management structure, rights, responsibilities, and financial arrangements.
Option	A legal right to purchase property at fixed terms during a specified window, without obligation. Used to control property for resale, renovation, or further structuring.
Option Agreement	A contract that grants one party the exclusive right, but not obligation, to purchase a property at predetermined terms within a specified time frame. Often used to control property while deferring purchase.

Term	Definition
Option Considera-tion	The payment made to the seller for the exclusive right to purchase under an option agreement. Typically, non-refundable and separate from rent.
Option Execution	The act of exercising the right to purchase granted in an option agreement. Converts a lease option into a binding sale contract.
Option Fee	(Same as Option Consideration; may differ in regional usage)
Option Period	The fixed window of time during which the buyer may exercise the option to purchase. Defined in the option agreement.
Origination Date	The date on which the loan was initially issued by the lender. Important for determining maturity, rate lock, and amortization status.
Origination Fee	A fee charged by a lender or broker to process and fund a loan. Typically expressed as a percentage of the loan amount.
Partial Wrap	A wraparound mortgage that finances only part of the underlying loan or purchase price. May involve combining seller financing with other funding sources.
Participation Model	he structure by which parties share profits, losses, decision-making, and risk. Common models include silent partnerships and sweat equity agreements.

Term	Definition
Passive Investor	An individual who supplies capital to a deal without taking part in management or operations. Typically expects periodic returns and final profit share.
Payment Stream	The flow of scheduled payments from buyer to seller, and from seller to the underlying lender. Managing this stream is essential to avoid default.
Performance Clause	A contractual term requiring one party to fulfill specific actions, such as maintaining lease payments. May trigger remedies if breached.
Power of Attorney	A legal authorization granting one party the authority to act on behalf of another. May be used to manage loan servicing or execute documents in subject-to transactions.
Preferred Return	A designated annual return rate distributed to investors before profits are split according to equity shares. Used to prioritize capital preservation.
Private Money	Capital provided by individuals, not institutions, for real estate investment. More flexible than bank financing, often based on relationship and asset.
Private Placement Memorandum	A legal disclosure document detailing the risks, terms, and structure of a private investment offering. Required for regulatory compliance.

Term	Definition
Promissory Note	A legal document in which a borrower commits to repay a specified sum under defined terms. In creative finance, seller-financed notes form the basis of many deals.
Purchase Price	The total consideration agreed upon by buyer and seller for the transfer of property. May include cash, notes, services, or other assets.
Recording Requirements	The legal obligations for documenting a real estate transaction with the county recorder.
Remedies for Default	The legal actions a seller may take upon buyer's failure to perform, such as eviction, forfeiture, or lawsuit for specific performance.
Rent Credit	A portion of lease payments applied toward the purchase price in a lease-option or lease-purchase structure. A flexible term used to build equity over time.
Risk Allocation	The distribution of transactional risks such as default, vacancy, or legal triggers among parties. Effective allocation protects clients and sustains deals.
Risk Management	The identification, evaluation, and mitigation of potential legal, financial, or ethical issues in a transaction. Brokers and agents must implement safeguards especially when employing non-standard deal structures.

Term	Definition
Risk Tolerance	An investor's capacity and willingness to endure variability or loss in investment performance. Used to match investor profiles to appropriate deal structures.
Sandwich Lease	A lease arrangement where the investor leases from the property owner and re-leases to a third party, profiting from the spread in terms.
Second Position	A subordinate lien recorded after a first mortgage or trust deed. Bears more risk and is paid only after senior debts.
Securities Compliance	Adherence to federal and state securities laws when raising capital or soliciting investors. Includes filing requirements and disclosure obligations.
Security Instrument	A document that creates a lien on the property to secure repayment of a loan. Typically, a mortgage or deed of trust.
Self-Directed IRA	A retirement account that allows investment in alternative assets, including real estate and notes, under IRS-compliant custodianship.
Seller Carryback	A financing strategy in which the seller of a property acts as the lender, carrying a promissory note secured by the property. Often used to bypass traditional mortgage underwriting.
Seller Financing	Same as Seller Carryback

Term	Definition
Seller Notification Risk	The legal and practical risk that the seller may alert the lender post-closing, potentially triggering the due-on-sale clause. Managed through disclosure and documentation.
Senior Lien	The primary or first position lien on a property. In a wraparound, this typically refers to the original mortgage loan being wrapped.
Silent Partner	A non-managing equity partner who contributes capital and receives profit share without involvement in daily operations.
Sourcing Funnel	The front-end process of identifying, qualifying, and capturing creative finance leads. May include marketing, referrals, and outbound outreach.
Sponsor	The individual or entity that identifies, structures, and manages an investment. In syndications, the sponsor often acts as the general partner.
Straight Note	A promissory note requiring periodic interest payments with principal due in a lump sum at maturity. Also known as an interest-only note.
Strike Price	The agreed-upon purchase price stated in an option agreement, regardless of future market changes. Defines the cost to exercise the option.

Term	Definition
Subject-To	A transaction structure where the buyer acquires property title while the seller's existing mortgage remains in place. The buyer agrees to make payments, but the loan stays in the seller's name.
Sublease	A secondary lease arrangement where the original lessee rents the property to another tenant. Must be permitted under the master lease.
Subordination Agreement	A legal document in which a lender agrees to maintain a lower priority than another lien. Sometimes used in wraps to protect title or improve risk posture.
Sweat Equity	Non-financial contribution to a venture, typically labor or expertise. Can create conflicts for licensees acting as both agent and principal.
Syndication	A structure where multiple investors pool capital to fund a real estate project or note investment, often managed by a sponsor or general partner.
Terms	The specific payment structure, timeline, and contingencies agreed upon in a transaction. Creative terms often involve flexibility around interest, timing, and performance conditions.
Title Company	A business that verifies property ownership, issues title insurance, and facilitates closing. Not all title companies are equipped to handle creative finance documents.

Term	Definition
Title Holding Period	The duration during which the seller retains legal title while the buyer pays under a contract for deed. Ends when title is conveyed.
Title Transfer	The legal conveyance of ownership rights from seller to buyer, typically executed through a deed. Timing may vary in creative finance structures.
Title Transfer Delay	Same as Title Holding Period
Underlying Loan	The original mortgage loan that remains on the property and is embedded into the wraparound arrangement. Its terms directly affect the structure of the wrap.
Voting Rights	Rights of members or partners to participate in governance decisions, as defined in the operating agreement.
Waterfall Distribution	A structured method of distributing profits among partners or investors based on tiers, such as return of capital, preferred return, and profit splits.
Wholesale Fee	A fee collected by assigning a lease-option or purchase contract to another buyer. Common monetization method in wholesaling.
Wholesaler	An unlicensed or licensed actor who secures real estate under contract and assigns that contract to a third-party buyer for a fee, typically without taking title or representing either party.

Term	Definition
Wholesaling	The practice of contracting to buy property and assigning that contract to another buyer for a fee, often without taking title. Heavily regulated and restricted for licensed agents in many jurisdictions.
Wrap	A financing structure where a new loan wraps around an existing one, allowing a seller or investor to create a note that includes the prior debt and earns a margin on the spread.
Yield	The income returned on an investment, typically expressed as a percentage of the capital invested. Includes interest, dividends, or rental income.